GRACED
—TO—
GOVERN

THE JOURNEY TO GROWTH BEGINS WITH GRACE
LEADERSHIP ANTHOLOGY

DR. DEBORAH C. ANTHONY
FOUNDING AUTHOR

Copyright © 2025 Dr. Deborah C. Anthony
King James Version (KJV) The King James Version (KJV) is in the public domain and does not require special permission for use. Copyright: Public Domain. New King James Version (NKJV) Scripture quotations taken from the New King James Version®. Copyright © 1982 by Thomas Nelson. Used by permission. All rights reserved. New International Version (NIV) Scripture quotations taken from The Holy Bible, New International Version®, NIV®. Copyright © 1973, 1978, 1984, 2011 by Biblica, Inc.® Used by permission. All rights reserved worldwide. English Standard Version (ESV) Scripture quotations are from The Holy Bible, English Standard Version® (ESV®), copyright © 2001 by Crossway, a publishing ministry of Good News Publishers. Used by permission. All rights reserved. New Living Translation (NLT) Scripture quotations are taken from the Holy Bible, New Living Translation, copyright © 1996, 2004, 2007, 2013 by Tyndale House Foundation. Used by permission of Tyndale House Publishers, Inc., Carol Stream, Illinois 60188. All rights reserved. World English Bible (WEB) The World English Bible is in the public domain and does not require permission for use. Copyright: Public Domain. Amplified Bible (AMP) Scripture quotations taken from the Amplified® Bible (AMP), copyright © 2015 by The Lockman Foundation, La Habra, CA 90631. All rights reserved. For Permission to Quote Information visit www.Lockman.org.

Graced to Govern
The Journey to Growth Begins with Grace

Dr. Deborah C. Anthony
deborah@deborahcanthony.com

ISBN 978-1-949027-04-4

Printed in the USA.
All rights reserved

Published by: Destined To Publish | Flossmoor, Illinois
www.DestinedToPublish.com

DEDICATION

You Are Graced to Govern

Leadership has always been necessary for a society to function. We see no greater model of leadership than that found in the Bible, both the Old and New Testaments. We also see that leaders were not chosen because they were perfect, they were chosen because God saw something in them that He wanted to use to help take His people from one place to another. This book is dedicated to those in leadership, assigned by God, to do a work for Him.

We want to encourage every leader who has ever questioned their calling, or felt overwhelmed by the weight of their assignment, or even grown weary. In this anthology you will not find the perfect people modeling leadership. Instead, you will find that God's grace guides imperfect people into His perfect plan to do a work for Him that impacts others.

Just as God spoke to Abram and called him to leave the familiar for the unknown, a unique grace is required to answer the divine call to leadership. Genesis 12:1–2 reminds us of God's words to Abram:

> *"Now the Lord had said unto Abram, Get thee out of thy country, and from thy kindred, and from thy father's house, unto a land that I will shew thee: And I will make of thee*

DEDICATION

a great nation, and I will bless thee, and make thy name great; and thou shalt be a blessing:" (KJV)

This faith journey requires trusting in His plan, even when the path is unclear. Through the pages of this anthology, my prayer is that you find renewed strength, divine clarity, and the courage to press forward in your calling. May this book inspire you to see God's hand in every step of your journey and embrace the grace that governs.

To the leaders who feel like giving up, remember: *"But they that wait upon the LORD shall renew their strength; they shall mount up with wings as eagles; they shall run, and not be weary; and they shall walk, and not faint"* (Isaiah 40:31, KJV).

May this book be a source of encouragement and empowerment, reminding you that God's grace is sufficient, and His strength is made perfect in our weakness. To every questioning soul, every weary heart, and every faltering hand, know that you are seen, loved, and equipped to lead with grace.

For the reader who seeks to wonder if there is a word from the Lord, the pages of this book come alive through the various testimonies and lived experiences that can transform your life through yielding to the greatest grace giver, our Lord and Savior Jesus Christ.

Press on, dear leader, for the work you do matters deeply to the Kingdom.

FOREWORD

Dr. Gaylena White
Pastor of Cutting Edge Global

You're about to journey through a collection of stories that underscores a fundamental truth: the path to authentic leadership begins with a journey of grace. As we grow in our understanding of God's love, we learn to govern our own hearts with compassion and integrity. We develop the humility to serve others, the wisdom to discern God's will, and the courage to lead with conviction and compassion.

Within these pages, you will encounter the heartfelt testimonies of individuals who, like you, have faced life's inevitable challenges. They are not tales of the effortlessly religious postures but rather honest and vulnerable accounts of how God's grace has sustained them through some of the toughest trials and triumphs. These stories share how trials, though painful, can purify our character and deepen our faith. They list how surrendering our will to God's leads to unexpected blessings and a life of profound peace. The honesty of each writer's struggles, both internal and external, fosters a genuine connection and opens the door to divine healing. And we even get to witness a miracle. The enduring hope of God's grace in these dark moments proves that God's love and mercy have graced us to prevail.

FOREWORD

My first introduction to many of these authors was right here in these pages, and I submit that I've been personally challenged and inspired. Revelations 12:11 says, *"And they overcame him by the blood of the Lamb and by the word of their testimony; and they loved not their lives unto the death"* (KJV). I'm so very grateful that these brave souls were transparent with their processes of being tried by fire. We will all now be able to overcome him without the battle but definitely by the blood. "Graced to Govern" is not merely a collection of anecdotes; it is a testament to the transformative power of God's Word.

These stories reveal how seemingly insurmountable obstacles—personal struggles, professional setbacks, and the weight of life's uncertainties—have become catalysts for growth. You will witness how these individuals, through the refiner's fire of prayer, perseverance, and a steadfast reliance on God's guidance, have learned to govern themselves with humility, honor, and a heart surrendered to His will with glorious outcomes! You just might cry until you laugh and vice versa; I did.

I pray these stories inspire you to view your own challenges not as insurmountable obstacles, but as opportunities for growth and refinement. May they encourage you to seek God's guidance in every circumstance, to trust in His unwavering love, and to embrace the journey of becoming the person He created you to be at all costs! Prepare to be challenged, encouraged, and deeply moved. Prepare to encounter the grace of God in the most unexpected places. Prepare to be "Graced to Govern" your life with wisdom, compassion, and a heart surrendered to His will.

With this dynamic series, you may now govern yourselves accordingly!

TABLE OF CONTENTS

Introduction 1

SPIRITUAL GROWTH

1. Graced with Power — *Dr. Maria Crawford* 15

2. Graced with Love — *Pastor Douglas Neal* 24

3. Graced to Abide — *Evangelist Tracie Vick* 34

FAMILY AND RELATIONSHIP

4. Graced to Follow God — *Drs. Hiram & Joronda Crawford* 47

5. Graced for Marriage — *Pastors Wesley & Neesha Stringfellow* 59

6. Grace to Parent — *Dr. Maria Crawford* 68

CHURCH AND LEADERSHIP

7. Graced for Success — *Bishop Stevie Jacobs* 75

8. Graced to Lead — *Minister Miyoshi Knox* 86

9. Graced for Purpose — *Apostle Michelle Kelly* 98

COMMUNITY AND SOCIETY

10. Graced to Care — *Pastor Jesus & Darcy Mateo* 107

11. Graced to Build — *Apostle Eleanor Stewart* 116

CHALLENGES AND GRIEF EMOTIONAL WELL-BEING

12. Graced to Pivot — *Apostle Dr. Crishanda Burgos* 129

13. Graced to Embrace Peace — *Pastor Miriam McFarland* 138

14. Graced to Land — *Elder Chandra Lace* 147

15. Graced to Endure — *Alexis Rose Lowry* 156

16. Graced to Grieve — *Dr. Deborah C Anthony* 166

GLOBAL PERSPECTIVE TO GOVERN

17. Graced for Counsel — *Apostle Sharlena Mack* 181

18. Graced to Distribute — *Apostle Dr. Kimberly McClinton* 189

19. Graced to Unify — *Prophetess Tracy Manning* 196

FUTURE HOPE AND ETERNAL PERSPECTIVE

20. Graced to Believe — *Pastor Kim Robinson* 207

21. Graced to Trust — *Kingdom Preneur Donna Lowry* 219

22. Graced to Wait — *Prophetess Tracy Smith* 232

23. Graced to Live — *Pastor Darrell Geddes* 244

24. Graced to Persevere — *Apostle Dr. Royal McClinton* 252

INTRODUCTION

Embracing Divine Governance Through Grace

Dr. Deborah C Anthony
FOUNDING AUTHOR

The quest for guidance and stability becomes increasingly pressing in a world brimming with complexities and ever-changing challenges. As believers navigating this tumultuous landscape, we are called not to anchor ourselves in the fleeting wisdom of the world but in the steadfast divine governance afforded by God's grace. The prophetic words of Isaiah lay a foundational truth for our journey:

> *"For unto us a child is born, unto us a son is given, and the government shall be upon his shoulder... Of the increase of his government and peace there shall be no end..."* (Isaiah 9:6-7, KJV).

INTRODUCTION

These verses herald the advent of Jesus Christ, upon whose shoulders rests the ultimate authority. His governance is neither temporal nor unstable; it is an everlasting rule, grounded in perfect righteousness. This divine proclamation underscores God's sovereign plan to guide and govern our lives through His Son, equipping us with wisdom, peace, and purpose, even when worldly systems falter.

Embracing this divine governance necessitates a profound recognition: we cannot do grace without God, nor can we approach God without grace. It is essential to understand that attempting life outside the realm of grace is futile, for nothing within us is inherently good enough to navigate life's trials alone. Through divine grace, we are not only sustained but also empowered to rise above the impermanence of earthly troubles firmly rooted in the eternal governance of Christ.

The Necessity of Divine Grace in Governance

Grace is more than unmerited favor; it is God's empowering presence enabling us to fulfill our divine purpose. Paul's words remind us that our identity and accomplishments are products of His grace at work in us: *"But by the grace of God I am what I am: and his grace which was bestowed upon me was not in vain..."* (1 Corinthians 15:10, KJV). Grace gives strength to overcome obstacles and the wisdom to choose righteousness. It infuses peace into our hearts, transcending earthly understanding: *"And the peace of God, which passeth all understanding, shall keep your hearts and minds through Christ Jesus"* (Philippians 4:7, KJV). With this divine wisdom, we can overcome life's challenges. Embracing God's grace is central to every aspect of our lives, preventing discouragement and confusion. The by-product is a peace that goes beyond our understanding. We trust His perfect will over our limited understanding by submitting to His governance. This submission renews our minds and realigns our priorities with His eternal purpose: *"And be not conformed to this world: but be ye transformed by the renewing of your mind..."* (Romans 12:2, KJV). Our very nature, which is bent toward self-satisfaction, necessitates the grace of God to govern our lives. It enables us to wait on Him and helps us trust His promises.

"The Government Shall Be Upon His Shoulder"

This phrase in Isaiah signifies the weight and responsibility of authority that Jesus carries. In ancient cultures, bearing a burden on one's shoulder indicated great importance. Christ, our Messiah, carries not just the governance of nations but our very lives as well. His rule is marked by justice, righteousness, and an unending peace: *"Of the increase of his government and peace, there shall be no end..."* (Isaiah 9:7, KJV). This truth compels us to relinquish our control and trust in His flawless leadership. We must ask ourselves: Who truly governs our decisions, relationships, and ambitions—self, society, or the sovereign King? Recognizing Christ's ultimate authority frees us from the tyranny of human standards and leads us into divine order. By following the government of God's kingdom, it ensures us that we can live the life God made us to live.

INTRODUCTION

Breaking Down Our Lives to Be Governed with Grace

To fully embrace God's governance through grace, we must examine the various life facets that need divine oversight. This anthology explores these areas, offering insights and practical guidance to live under the gentle rule of God's government. Each area of life represents an opportunity for God's grace to bring alignment, healing, and direction.

Spiritual Growth

Our journey begins with the heart. Spiritual maturity flourishes when grace transforms us from within: *"But grow in grace, and in the knowledge of our Lord and Saviour Jesus Christ..."* (2 Peter 3:18, KJV). *Daily* surrender, engagement with Scripture, and intimacy with God are essential: *"Abide in me, and I in you..."* (John 15:4, KJV).

By remaining connected to Christ, we draw from His strength, navigate life from a divine perspective, and bear eternal fruit. Galatians 2:20 says: *I am crucified with Christ: nevertheless, I live; yet not I, but Christ liveth in me: and the life which I now live in the flesh I live by the faith of the Son of God, who loved me, and gave himself for me* (KJV).

Family and Relationships

Grace governs how we love, forgive, and serve our family. It strengthens marriages: *"Husbands, love your wives, even as Christ also loved the church, and gave himself for it and the wives see that she reverence her husband"* (Ephesians 5:25, KJV). It guides us to raise children in the Lord's instruction: *"And, ye fathers, provoke not your children to wrath: but bring them up in the nurture and admonition of the Lord"* (Ephesians 6:4, KJV). Christ's love sets the standard: *"A new commandment I give unto you, that ye love one another; as I have loved you..."* (John 13:34, KJV).

When grace governs our relationships, homes become sanctuaries of mercy, understanding, and spiritual growth. Our contemporary culture has led many of us away from these simple teachings. As a result, divorce and single parent homes are becoming the norm, not the exception. There is no easy solution to the crisis that the family is facing. Prayer, sound teaching, and counseling are all needed to mend broken families and instruct new families how to live with one another.

Work and Vocation

In our professional life, grace shapes ethics, diligence, and how we interact with colleagues: *"And whatsoever ye do, do it heartily, as to the Lord, and not unto men..."* (Colossians 3:23, KJV).

Working as unto the Lord infuses meaning into mundane tasks and transforms the workplace into a mission field of integrity and excellence. The workplace has changed in many ways, however, no matter what the industry, there is a scramble for power positions. Leadership classes abound, with so many aspiring to be leaders, and not many wanting to settle to be the workers. Jesus showed us how to be in leadership, and it is totally opposite from the teachings of this world. Jesus showed His authority by serving. He said: *"...whosoever will be great among you, let him be your servant;"* (Matthew 20: 26, KJV). When we understand the goal is not to be the one in charge, rather to contribute what God has assigned us to do, we prosper in the thing that He sent us to do, whatever the capacity. We can thus be content in the board room or the mail room.

Community and Society

As Christ's ambassadors, we influence communities with justice, mercy, and humility: *"He hath shewed thee, O man, what is good; and what doth the LORD require of thee, but to do justly, and to love mercy, and to walk humbly with thy God?"* (Micah 6:8, KJV).

By being salt and light: *"Ye are the light of the world..."* (Matthew 5:14, KJV), we address social issues with compassion, offering hope amidst turmoil and guiding others toward righteousness. We no longer sit in the seat of judgement, determining whether someone is worthy of social status. Rather, we see each human being as one that God made, on purpose and for purpose; and if we have intervened with them, it gives us the opportunity to love them to their next place in God.

Challenges and Temptations

Life's trials test faith and character. Grace strengthens us to endure temptations: *"There hath no temptation taken you, but such as is common to man: but God is faithful..."* (1 Corinthians 10:13, KJV).

We count trials as joy, knowing they produce perseverance: *"My brethren, count it all joy when ye fall into divers' temptations; Knowing this, that the trying of your faith worketh patience."* (James 1:2-3, KJV).

INTRODUCTION

Grace keeps us steadfast, even refining our faith through adversity. Adversity not only refines our faith but produces the means for the fruit of the spirit to develop in our lives. Each test and challenge builds our spiritual muscles, gives us compassion for others, and perfects weak areas within us.

Emotional and Mental Well-being

Mental health is integral to our overall wellness. Grace offers healing for broken hearts: *"He healeth the broken in heart, and bindeth up their wounds"* (Psalm 147:3, KJV). Peace for anxious minds: *"Casting all your care upon him; for he careth for you"* (1 Peter 5:7, KJV). And comfort in dark valleys: *"Yea, though I walk through the valley of the shadow of death, I will fear no evil: for thou art with me..."* (Psalm 23:4, KJV).

God's grace gives us solace, strength, and renewed hope. There is no one outside of the need for fellowship. There are even times as scripture affirms that: *"In the multitude of counselors there is safety"* (Proverbs 11:14, KJV).

Stewardship and Finances

All resources come from God. Grace teaches faithful stewardship: *"If therefore ye have not been faithful in the unrighteous mammon, who will commit to your trust the true riches?"* (Luke 16:11, KJV). We give cheerfully, trusting God's provision: *"Every man according as he purposeth in his heart, so let him give; not grudgingly, or of necessity: for God loveth a cheerful giver"* (2 Corinthians 9:7, KJV).

This stewardship influences how we invest our time, talents, and resources for His glory. There has never been a time when learning the principles of stewardship has been more important, not only for our personal sake, but also to be able to share these principles with our children.

Global Perspective and Missions

The Great Commission calls us to go beyond our borders. Grace compels us to share the gospel worldwide: *"Go ye therefore and teach all nations..."* (Matthew 28:19, KJV). We develop a global mindset, encouraging cultures to embrace the Kingdom's transformative power. The world is now where there is no where you cannot reach in a day either through air travel or satellite; going into all the world is an attainable challenge.

Church and Fellowship

The body of Christ thrives when grace governs interactions, fostering unity: *"Endeavouring to keep the unity of the Spirit in the bond of peace"* (Ephesians 4:3, KJV). Spiritual gifts flourish under grace: *"Having then gifts differing according to the grace that is given to us..."* (Romans 12:6, KJV). In such an environment, the church reflects Christ's love and effectively represents Him on earth. We need each other. The church is the place that God ordained for us to receive the kind of fellowship that we need. It also provides a schoolhouse, where we learn to work out our salvation, through working with one other.

INTRODUCTION

Future Hope and Eternal Perspective

Our hope is anchored in eternity. Grace shifts our focus from temporary struggles to eternal promises: *"While we look not at the things which are seen, but at the things which are not seen: for the things which are seen are temporal; but the things which are not seen are eternal"* (2 Corinthians 4:18, KJV). We await Christ's return with anticipation: *"Looking for that blessed hope, and the glorious appearing of the great God and our Saviour Jesus Christ..."* (Titus 2:13, KJV). This eternal perspective motivates us to live out our purpose, assured that our labor in the Lord is never in vain.

Setting the Stage for Transformation

As we enter subsequent chapters, our goal is to reveal how God's grace, allowed to govern, transforms our lives completely. Contributors from diverse backgrounds share insights and testimonies, each demonstrating the profound impact of divine governance.

A world championing self-governance often leads to anxiety and emptiness. By contrast, submitting to God's rule yields peace, direction, and fulfillment unknown to worldly systems. *"Trust in the LORD with all thine heart; and lean not unto thine own understanding. In all thy ways acknowledge him, and he shall direct thy paths"* (Proverbs 3:5-6, KJV). One day we will join with Christ to live forever and ever. Until that time, while we walk this earthly terrain, God has afforded us the opportunity to experience miracles, wonders and signs that go beyond anything that our natural mind could imagine.

INTRODUCTION

Challenges to Embracing Divine Governance

It's one thing to acknowledge the necessity of needing grace; living it out is another. We face internal struggles—pride, fear, doubt: *"For the good that I would I do not: but the evil which I would not, that I do"* (Romans 7:19, KJV). And external pressures from a culture opposing godly principles: *"And be not conformed to this world: but be ye transformed by the renewing of your mind..."* (Romans 12:2a, KJV).

These forces challenge God's rightful place as Governor of our existence. This anthology does not shy away from these truths but offers biblical solutions and encouragement. Through scripture, testimony, and practical application, we confront and overcome barriers to living under grace.

Dear reader, journey with us through these pages. Allow the Holy Spirit to reveal areas in your life that need surrender, healing, and/or realignment. Embracing divine governance isn't a one-time choice but a daily walk with our Savior. *"And he said to them all, If any man will come after me, let him deny himself, and take up his cross daily, and follow me"* (Luke 9:23, KJV). Reflect on who governs your choices. Reevaluate where self or society leads you astray. Recommit to God's grace as your guiding force.

Isaiah's prophecy assures a never-ending government and peace under Christ's lordship: *"...to order it, and to establish it with judgment and with justice from henceforth even for ever..."* (Isaiah 9:7, KJV).

Submitting to His governance allows us to participate in His divine plan and experience the abundant life He promises: *"The thief cometh not, but for to steal, and to kill, and to destroy: I come that they might have life, and that they might have it more abundantly"* (John 10:10, KJV).

This anthology is more than a collection of writings; it's a clarion call to embrace the transformative power of God's grace in this governance. May it guide you toward a deeper intimacy with God, a life radiating His glory, and the fulfillment of His eternal purposes. *"And the peace of God, which passeth all understanding, shall keep your hearts and minds through Christ Jesus."* (Philippians 4:7, KJV). As we embark on this journey together, let us step into the abundant life that awaits us when we allow grace to govern.

SPIRITUAL GROWTH

1

GRACED WITH POWER

Gentle Power

Dr. Maria Crawford

The words of Jesus:

> *So Jesus called them together and said, "You know that the rulers in this world lord it over their people, and officials flaunt their authority over those under them. But among you, it will be different. Whoever wants to be a leader among you must be your servant, and whoever wants to be first among you must be the slave of everyone else. For even the Son of Man came not to be served but to serve others and to give his life as a ransom for many." (Mark 10:42-45, KJV)*

We live in a world that is consumed with power. While the picture may come to your mind of nations trying to exert power and authority over another nation or a political party winning over another party, today's concept of power is much more complex. For today, the word "power" could also be translated "influencer". People want to exert authority over others, through mental and emotional power, influencing their thinking and behavior. The quest for power and influence, though subtle, has had a profound effect upon our society. Recent studies report that social media has created a culture that has produced up to 75% of its' followers having a poor self-image. The severity of the impact upon individuals has developed into increasing numbers of so many of those followers' experiencing depression and even self-harm.

Jesus had a solution for those who wanted to rise to public popularity or ascend to power. It was not to look at the latest trendsetter and mimic them; rather, it was to take up a towel and a basin and begin to serve someone; in his day to wash their feet. His solution was to extend help to those who had a need—the sick, the poor, and the vulnerable. To look around and see the troubled, the weak, and the worn. If we want to identify with a real power broker, like unto our Lord and Savior Jesus Christ, we must serve - not rule and reign.

> *"And Jesus came and spake unto them, saying, all power is given unto me in heaven and in earth."* (Matthew 28:18, KJV)

Jesus was born the Son of God and the Son of man. It was evident while He walked the earth that He had the ability to heal, deliver, and set free. Yet in this passage, Jesus wanted to reinforce that with the completion of His earthly assignment, His assignment on earth did not reduce His influence or power; rather, it was established to a greater degree. He assumed the position of King of Kings and Lord of Lords with the capacity to influence the whole world!

Jesus never took up a sword, nor even fought with His hands. Jesus, like His Father, used words to shape His power. He spoke, and it happened. *"He called things that were not as though they were"* (Romans 4:17, KJV), and they became. This is what I call power, not power from a violent overthrow. It is gentle power. It does not need fanfare to herald its coming; it moves quietly but effectively to accomplish its' task.

As Jesus taught His disciples, He issued this directive:

> *"He sat down, called the twelve disciples over to him, and said, 'Whoever wants to be first must take last place and be the servant of everyone else.'"* (Mark 9:35, KJV)

At a time in Israel's history when kings ruled over them and soldiers surrounded and monitored their every move, the above passage was no doubt hard to digest. After all, the children of Israel had looked for hundreds of years for a Messiah to come and deliver them from all foreign oppression. That thought was intensified during the years Jesus walked the earth, for while the disciples believed that Jesus exhibited signs that He was the Son of God, they also wondered when He would begin to deliver them from Roman rule. There is no doubt they experienced a great deal of conflict in their hearts.

While we don't have kings or even soldiers ruling over us, there is a more ostentatious form of power that men rule with. It's an everyday occurrence. We go to jobs where there are different grades of positions. There are those who "do" and those who tell others what to "do". Given the choice, most of us would rather be in the position of telling others what to do. This is human nature. However, those types of positions are not as accessible as the ones who just "do". To aspire to leadership positions that give us power, there is often a process that involves getting the attention of those in the supreme level of authority. Here is the caveat: you are not usually noticed because you serve; your leadership ability is more readily observed if you yield the kind of influence over others by getting them to do what you want them to do.

The secular world is very different from the Kingdom of God. Jesus said that *"those who want to be first must take the last place and be the servant of all"* (Mark 9:35, KJV). How then can a Christian rise to a leadership position on their job if they called to a place of serving? Who will notice them? This is a good question, and it is easily answered. Your corporate executive leader may never notice your acts of service, but he is not your ultimate boss. As a believer, we are in this world, but not of this world. Our life is governed by the highest authority of all—that is our Father, God. God sees, God knows, God cares. When we operate according to the dictates that Jesus gave us, we find that Psalm 75:6-7 is true:

> *"For promotion cometh neither from the east, nor from the west, nor from the south. But God is the judge: he putteth down one, and setteth up another."* (KJV)

It is God, our Father, who ultimately places us in the positions that He desires. He will direct a path for us that will take us to places *"exceedingly and abundantly above all we can ask or even think"* (Ephesians 3:20, KJV). True power lies in submitting to the Lordship of Jesus Christ. It is steeped in "a wisdom that comes from heaven [that] *is first of all pure; then peace-loving, considerate, submissive, full of mercy and good fruit, impartial and sincere"* (James 3:17, KJV). In other words, it is a kind of gentle power that moves in a way that not only affects you but those around you. As power brokers examine your life, they become curious as to how you are experiencing promotion without using the typical antics that others do.

I have seen this in my own life. While going about my job in the public sector as a servant, I have been asked on more than one occasion to take leadership roles that I never even applied for. The positions afforded me the opportunity to influence the culture of the organization in a quiet way—not by lording over people, but by showing by example how we could better help our clients by being a servant!

One instance comes to mind. I had begun a master's degree program in administration. One day I felt prompted to write down what I felt was the best job I could aspire to. What followed was months of one challenge after another. From all indication, that job was never going to happen. In fact, I even was downsized where I had been working.

I got another job, and it seemed like this was the worst place I had ever worked at. Little did I know that the way I dealt with the challenges I faced was not going unnoticed. Fast forward six months and I had the job that I had written down that day six months prior. I must confess that no one was more surprised than I was. And what was my job: serving my superior, and serving the students, parents, teachers and surrounding community in the school that I worked for.

When we have become vested as a believer and know "who we are" and "whose we are", we understand that we have all of heaven backing us. Philippians 2:5-7 says:

> *"Let this mind be in you, which was also in Christ Jesus: Who, being in the form of God, thought it not robbery to be equal with God: But made himself of no reputation, and took upon him the form of a servant, and was made in the likeness of men:"* (KJV)

By following Jesus' example, we begin to operate in the marketplace a different way. We learn that the love that God gives to us, we can give to others. We learn we do not have to prove ourselves, that the wisdom from God, steeped in righteousness, will always direct us to take the right path. We find that complex problems are easily solved when we seek the wisdom from above. We know that when the victory comes, the real winner is not us, but all glory goes to God. However, we also see the fruit of that victory is spread around so that everyone benefits from it. It is tragic that so few take advantage of the life-giving, life-sustaining, life-affirming power of God. Those who do soon find out that *"the blessings of the Lord are rich and add no sorrow"* (Proverbs 10:22, KJV).

Now, I would not be portraying the whole story without stating that these blessings come with persecutions:

> *"And Jesus answered and said, Verily I say unto you, there is no man that hath left house, or brethren, or sisters, or father, or mother, or wife, or children, or lands, for my sake, and the gospel's,*
>
> *But he shall receive a hundredfold now in this time, houses, and brethren, and sisters, and mothers, and children, and lands, **with persecutions;** and in the world to come eternal life. But many that are first shall be last; and the last first."* (Mark 10:29-31, KJV)

On our journey of life, we will find times and seasons when we must leave the 'safe route', to walk down an unknown course. It might mean taking an unpopular stand, or taking a lesser role, even when there is a chance to do otherwise. When we hear the voice of God leading us, others around us may not understand. Undoubtedly, we receive advice that is always contrary to what we hear God saying. We have a choice: we can follow God's voice, or we can yield to popular opinion.

When we choose to follow God's voice, the path may be rocky; there undoubtedly will be enemies on the road trying to discourage us from continuing the chosen path. Our family and friends may taunt us by saying, *"I told you this wasn't the way."* Those are the kinds of persecutions that Jesus was talking about. However, in the above passage, we also see a promise, and that promise is what we can count on: *"no man has left…for my sake, and the gospels, but he shall receive a hundredfold now in this time… and in the world to come eternal life."*

This is what we call a surety note. We can count on it.

So, what do we have to lose? On Good Friday, it looked like everything was over; Jesus was finished. His strange new doctrine seemed to have failed Him. Yet, three days later, there was an empty tomb. Jesus had triumphed over death, and not only did He gain a king's crown, but He captured the keys to death and hell and made it possible for everyone who believes on Him to have the right to eternal life. With His victory, He also got **"all power"**—not having to do with swords and spears, but a gentle encompassing power that says:

> *"But thank God! He has made us his captives and continues to lead us along in Christ's triumphal procession. Now he uses us to spread the knowledge of Christ everywhere, like a sweet perfume."* (2 Corinthians 2:14, KJV)

What a glorious promise! Thus, we look upon persecutions not as the end, but as a part of the process that enables us to become overcomers. We understand that tests and trials will come, but along with that is *"life and that more abundantly"*. The assurances that the Bible gives us, indicates that we will have ultimate victory while on this earth, and the glorious promise of life eternally with Jesus. Let us never weary of serving the King of all Kings, the One who exhibits - *Gentle Power!*

Dr. Maria Crawford, a retired educator, has served youth and young adults in both public and Christian education. Her passion for teaching continues as she leads Bible studies and contributes to the spiritual formation of this next generation including her 29 grand and 8 great grandchildren. She writes frequently for HeartLifeToday.com.

2

GRACED WITH LOVE

Loving People to Their Next Place in God
Pastor Douglas Neal

Destinations are often exciting to look forward to. Taking the kids to Disney World, a romantic getaway to a tropical island, a reflective hike through a mountain range, or a holiday visit with family and friends…It's an invigorating feeling when we anticipate the wonder of our "next place."

That's why it greatly intrigued my wife and I when the Lord spoke to her concerning the tagline of our church – Loving People to Their NEXT PLACE in God. The phrasing felt right to us, and we couldn't explain why. As we pondered and prayed over it more, a few things about it began to stand out.

Though it's not directly stated, this phrase implies that we are meeting people where they are, regardless of where that may be – in the best of godly places or in the worst of sinful places. It is intended to reflect what God did for mankind. He saw the brokenness of our lives and decided to become fully man while remaining fully God to meet us where we are.

God's purpose for coming into this world in the form of our Savior Jesus Christ was not to condemn us but to save us. Jesus makes this plain in His clandestine meeting with Nicodemus in John 3. Jesus says to Nicodemus in verse 17, *"God sent his Son into the world not to judge the world, but to save the world through him"* (KJV).

This greatly challenges our natural inclination to point out the negative attributes of humanity, including our own. We see the burgeoning of this broken mindset from the beginning of creation. The onset of sin clearly distorted man's perspective of himself and others and made it difficult to see God's glory in human creation. Instead, we became relegated to faultfinding and judgment.

In Genesis 3, the serpent deceives the woman, Eve, into eating fruit from the forbidden tree that God explicitly instructed her and the man, Adam, not to eat of, lest they surely die. The instant that this happened, they immediately saw their nakedness. They saw themselves and each other as deficient, insufficient, inadequate, broken, and out-of-order. Worse than this, they saw each other as the blame for the problem.

The idea of loving people to their next place in God demands a renewed perspective of people. It first requires "LOVING PEOPLE…" The words from the epistle of James come to mind.

In chapter 3, James speaks of how crucial yet how difficult it is to control our tongues. He describes it as a body organ "full of deadly poison". James 3:8-10 says,

> *But the tongue can no man tame; it is an unruly evil, full of deadly poison. Therewith bless we God, even the Father; and therewith curse we men, which are made after the similitude of God. Out of the same mouth proceedeth blessing and cursing. My brethren, these things ought not so to be.* (KJV)

This is important to note because Jesus says in Matthew 12:34 that *"out of the abundance of the heart, the mouth speaks"* (KJV). The deadly poison of the tongue stems directly from the heart of man – a heart corrupted by sin to see only the negative broken aspects of others.

Our deluded hearts do not naturally perceive "the image of God" as prescribed by the Apostle James. When we look at each other, we see through the veil of our tainted lens, and we see only the flaws, mistakes, and imperfections of sinful humanity. As a result, we treat one another according to the shortcomings we interpret.

Rarely do our interactions with others overtly express this negative viewpoint of humanity. However, we often sense the undercurrent of judgment and criticism towards and from others. Nevertheless, Jesus clearly admonishes us not to judge others. He says in Matthew 7:1-2, *"Do not judge others, and you will not be judged. For you will be treated as you treat others. The standard you use in judging is the standard by which you will be judged"* (NLT).

From all of this, we can conclude that an important key to "LOVING PEOPLE" is seeing people through God's lens. If this is the case, then we need God to renew our hearts, leading to a new perspective of mankind. This begs the question, "How does God see people?"

To love people to their next place in God requires us to see people how God sees people. There is no level of our salvation or natural understanding that can fully encapsulate God's perspective of man (or anything else for that matter). Yet there are plenty of verses in the Bible that indicate the depth God's love for all of us.

One of my personal favorites comes from Romans 5:8, which says that *"God showed his great love for us by sending Christ to die for us while we were still sinners"* (NLT). The prior verses in this chapter delineate that scarcely will people die for a righteous person. Yet conversely, Jesus died for us while we were at our absolute worst.

This is the heart of our tagline. We meet people where they are and no matter how vile or off-putting their past or present lifestyles have been, we determine by the power of God through His transformative power in our hearts to first LOVE them.

Every person we encounter will be at a different place. So, there is no cookie cutter method to love them to their next place. We must fight the temptation of trying to entreat people according to how we entreat others. Different people have different needs. Taking time to get to know individuals helps to guide us to effective ways of loving them to their next place in God.

When our hearts are transformed to the place of being able to receive people as they are, we then focus our attention on how to help them from where they are to where they need to be. It should be noted that we are not trying to help people to their next place in our church culture. In fact, many of the people we encounter are likely to have come out of such environments and have no need to return.

Our goal is to help people see and experience God through His Word and by the power of His Spirit and not the repetition of our own church or spiritual experience. We are not loving people to OUR former place in God. We're loving them to THEIR next place in God.

People have been on different journeys and have taken different paths. Their next place may require the guidance of someone with similar experience that may be very different than what you have. In either case, people need to feel the welcome from believers without the pressure to move in a certain direction or pace.

However, this doesn't mean that such guidance isn't without confrontation. I don't mean the aggressive brand of confrontation that demands that people instantly change to what we think they ought to be. I mean giving people a loving opportunity to take an honest look at themselves and truthfully acknowledging how far they are from the life God desires for them.

There are several areas in our lives that the Bible underscores this need for growth. One is the aspect of "purpose". Another word for this is "calling". The Apostle Paul says in Philippians 3:14, *"I press on to reach the end of the race and receive the heavenly prize for which God, through Christ Jesus, is calling us"* (NLT).

God is always calling us to a higher place in Him and in His purpose for us. This is the latter portion of the tagline of loving people to their next place in God. God has a place and a purpose for everyone. It is a very fulfilling occurrence to find that next place of purpose but it's even more fulfilling to help others to find it for themselves.

A calling requires the ability to hear. There are several places in the Bible where the phrase, *"He that has an ear, let him hear what the Spirit says to the churches"*, can be found. Hearing the voice of the Lord calling us means first having a relationship with God through salvation in Christ Jesus.

Once we have given our lives to Christ, the Holy Spirit helps us to hear God's voice. It's important to realize that the Holy Spirit always agrees with the Word of God. So, knowing the Word is equally as important as having the Holy Spirit when it comes to hearing God and answering His calling.

Not everyone has an ear developed well enough to clearly hear what God is saying to them. Having a desire to help others hear God clearly doesn't necessarily mean that we have such an ear that hears clearly either. Many times, however, it can be easier to see from the outside having a fresh perspective that can give others insight to what God is calling them to do.

Another area in the next place in our lives where the need for growth applies is in our gifting. While we all have something that God has called us to do, it's important to realize that God has gifted us to accomplish it. Both in Romans 12 and in 1 Corinthians 12, the Apostle Paul accentuates how God has gifted each of us.

Not only do we all have gifts, but our gifts also come in a wide variety. As we help others to discover their gifts, we must also point out how important it is to make our gifts work together to accomplish the greater work of the Lord. No gift is more important than the other. Thus, it takes great humility to walk in the unity that is needed to make gifts work together.

In truth, we really cannot fulfill our calling without help from the rest of the gifts. In the same way each part of our bodies needs the other, our gifts need to work together with other gifts to accomplish God's will and purpose for our lives. As 1 Corinthians 12 remits, the whole body is not about one singular function. The whole body is not made for hearing or for seeing. All the parts work together and support one another. Helping each other to remember this is another way that we love people to their next place.

Romans 11:29 says that the *"gifts and the calling of God are irrevocable"* (NIV). God does not change His mind about how He created us or what He created us for. There is no greater hindrance from seeing our calling through, than a lifestyle of sin. Sin can literally be the death of our purpose.

As Paul says in Romans 6:23, *"… the wages of sin is death"* (KJV). Sin can certainly cause actual death, but it can also cause death to many other things in our lives, such as relationships, marriages, business ventures, ministries, and many other things in our lives that we value. This is why loving people to their next place in God is not without confrontation.

Galatians 6: 1 instructs us, *"that if another believer is overcome by some sin, you who are godly should gently and humbly help that person back onto the right path. And be careful not to fall into the same temptation yourself"* (NLT). The key words here are "gently" and "humbly".

Anytime we see someone on the wrong path, we have a responsibility to help them back onto the right one. But we need to remember the life we once lived. None of us have lived perfect sinless lives. We can all relate to other people's struggles with sin.

No one likes to be corrected. In this age, we can sense the unrelenting stance of independence. The minute we acknowledge where someone is going in the wrong direction, we can easily become a target of being labeled as judgmental.

Nevertheless, we all need accountability. We need people in our lives that we can trust to help us back to where we need to be without shame or condemnation. This is why Paul instructs us to be humble and gentle in our approach to love people back onto a path of righteousness.

Each of these areas play its' part in the primary reason of why these things are necessary. It is to display the glorious splendor of God to the rest of the world. Individuals in the body of Christ are like puzzle pieces. Each piece brings a different part of the whole picture to life. No piece is effective at displaying this picture alone. Being isolated from each other is never a successful strategy to bring the purpose and plan of God to life.

To display the full picture, all the puzzle pieces must come together. But they can't just be placed in any random place. Each piece must be properly placed together with the piece that matches what they are displaying. Each person must know where they fit, for It then takes time to know where the other "pieces" among us fit.

When we come together in our right places, a beautiful picture of what God has designed becomes visible to the rest of the world.

In John 17, Jesus expresses how important our unity is to help the world see God's glory.

Here's a look at verses 21-23:

> *I pray that they will all be one, just as you and I are one— as you are in me, Father, and I am in you. And may they be in us so that the world will believe you sent me. "I have given them the glory you gave me, so they may be one as we are one. I am in them, and you are in me. May they experience such perfect unity that the world will know that you sent me and that you love them as much as you love me.* (NIV)

Loving people to their next place in God is quite the undertaking. Helping people to hear the voice of God calling them, understanding their gifts, graciously steering them back onto the right path, and doing it all with gentleness and humility takes the power of God working in us. We need God's love and grace to help others draw closer to God.

No matter what background, culture, or lifestyle people come from, everyone needs help moving forward into the place where God has called them. The love and support we give them to get to that next place can make all the difference in their lives. As people come to know their piece of the puzzle, they can put them together with others that the world can clearly see and choose God for themselves.

Pastor Doug Neal is a Friends International Masters graduate in Biblical Studies. He and his wife, Shanna, serve as pastors of Christian Life Center South Bend. Parents of three adult children, Doug and Shanna have a passionate drive to foster and promote unity throughout the body of Christ.

3

GRACED TO ABIDE

Abiding With Intention
Evangelist Tracie Vick

"Abide in me, and I in you. As the branch cannot bear fruit of itself, except it abide in the vine; no more can ye, except ye abide in me." (John 15:4, KJV)

The message version states *"Live in me. Make your home in me just as I do in you. In the same way that a branch can't bear grapes by itself but only by being joined to the vine, you can't bear fruit unless you are joined with me" (*John 15:4, MSG).

Wow, the message version is clear on how God wants us to abide in Him. I had it all wrong. I knew I needed to yield every area of my life to God. Even the hidden me. It was time!

What does abiding mean to you? For me it is obedience. It is being purposeful, intentional, dwelling in God's presence, having a covenant relationship with our Father. When people see you, they should see God in you. Honestly, for many years I had never reflected on this, in this manner. Living in a world that has been inundated with modernization has prompted numerous souls to be led astray, hence being plucked in the mayhem of life. Therefore, I have to say that, not abiding with intentionality has been what occurred in my life. I became so complacent with the world, feeling that this is just how it is, and you must roll with the punches. I honestly believed that I was making things happen on my own strength and didn't need help from anyone. I thought I had this thing figured out. Whew, I was WRONG!

Life is like a spinning volcano with individuals trying to surface to the top of it and reach what is known as the crater, this is the opening at the top of the volcano. Those who are chasing a bag as they say, trying to climb the ladder and obtain fame, etc. are trying to reach the crater, not knowing that this is extremely dangerous as there could at any point be an eruption. When we are in a hurry to get what we want by any means necessary or to climb to the top on our own accord, detonation can occur. This is just how life is sometimes. We want something so bad; we are almost willing to sell our souls to obtain it.

Let me give you an example out of my personal experience. I married in June of 2001 to my first husband. After receiving warnings by way of prophecy that I was not to marry him, because this indeed was not my husband. I ignored them and went forth with the marriage. The marriage was a tsunami waiting to happen because 90% of the time, we did not even like one another. We could not get along at all. We conceived three beautiful children, one son and two daughters. But outside of that we were both miserable. We were forcing a puzzle to fit that was never meant to. In our disobedience, we did not get to choose our consequences.

I found myself a single mother, something I had never envisioned for my life. I wanted more in life and yet I wanted to satisfy my fleshly desires. I met someone through mutual friends, and I was in pursuit of this individual as if I was some desperate woman. The ink wasn't even dry on the divorce papers. You see, I was so adamant on fulfilling my need of not being lonely that I never turned back to God. I operated solely in my flesh. I finally convinced the guy to hang out with me. We were drinking and I used manipulation to get what I wanted.

Fast forward to surrendering my life to God completely, the Holy Spirit reminded me of this. Now I was wondering, God why is this resurfacing? We have a way of suppressing our traumatic experiences, so we can disguise or mask our pain. This is exactly what I did. As a little girl I was heartbroken when my dad moved out, and five years later at the age of fifteen, my brother died while playing basketball, then years later after I was an adult, I lost my son. I didn't realize what this would do to me as an adult. I had trust issues with men. I had to stay in control of every situation in my life because I thought I could control the outcomes. When I surrendered to God, everything hidden began to unfold. God needed to unveil the hidden me to ME, and it literally knocked\ the wind out of me. I was taught that a breaking had to occur before a breakthrough could emerge. Yet I didn't realize what that breaking would entail. I soon realized that I couldn't govern in God's kingdom, by putting on a false front.

God took this opportunity to reveal so much to me. He highlighted how I had relied on the spirit of manipulation, rather than the Holy Spirit. Many of us are not abiding with the intention to serve God, but rather with a controlling spirit. I realized that the resurfacing of my past was not to hurt me, nor to embarrass me, but to stretch me. God had given me unlimited grace to govern as I had suffered well, even when I wasn't cognitive of it, and I was just going through the motions. It is only by the grace of God that I am still standing.

You see, there was a need that had to be met, and to be met under God's authority. That need entailed being all in. I remember the first time I heard an amazing woman of God, Apostle Crishanda Burgos say, "Suffer Well' and I instantly thought, how is this possible? I was perplexed. What does she mean? And when she told me that I had a Peter Anointing, I instantly got offended. Like many people, I suffered from negating the message when it did not sound like I wanted to hear it. This is how we often miss God. Although, my first thought was how Peter betrayed Jesus, and I said, "that's not me"! God immediately reminded me of how I betrayed Him by indulging in my worldly desires. When He spoke to me and I said, "not yet God".

Then He proceeded to show up in other ways, through strangers and yet I said, "No". I sat there completely dumbstruck as this hit me hard. The truth often strikes a mighty blow, but it is a much-needed blow. I began to ruminate on how I felt so loved. God loved me so much, even when I told Him no, He chased me down. This is the kind of love I had never experienced before. As a matter a fact, no human has the capacity to love like this. Now, I ran to God, full speed ahead. I couldn't breathe without Him. He is my air, and I was ready to let God lead. My posture became, "Send me Lord, even if I must stand alone, I'll GO."

I began to sit before God and began to get in His word to understand just how to sustain. The first major revelation was how Jesus suffered on the cross without so much as an iota of a complaint. He was the epitome of "suffering well." God then reminded me of everything I had endured: inherited trauma, self-inflicted trauma, consequences because of my disobedience, my bad choices, my jezebel manipulative spirit, my uncontrolled anger, the words packed with venom that would come from my mouth; the murderous spirit I was consumed with when I lost my son, and I wanted to retaliate. The betrayal of family members who molested other family members, and so much more. Although anger arose repeatedly and tried to consume me, and I could not stray, I knew that without God I would not survive.

This required me to submerge into the word to reach the root of it all, every area of my life to uproot it, recognizing that it would become a deadly poison the more potent it is. Our traumatic experiences are not our fault in most cases. Some however are because we are given free will by God, so when we make our choices out of His will for our lives, we do not get to choose our consequences.

As a young girl and preteen, the church we attended was focused on prosperity. The churches we attended were focused more on the cross, and not Jesus. I remembered going to visit a church with a family friend and her children, and it was completely different from what I had experienced. There was praise and worship. I knew I wanted, no, I needed, I craved a covenant relationship with God. Soaking in the presence of God. I wanted to wear God like a luxurious garment. I wanted people to see God when they saw me. I wanted to be all in, I needed to be all in. There could be no more part time, convenient, or out of obligation relationship with God.

> *"But you do not have His word abiding in you, because whom He sent, Him do not believe."* (John 5:38, NKJV)

When I accepted the call of Evangelism on my life, one thing I knew is that I would go out and bring souls to Christ. I love the righteous church, but I know that I am called to go out among the lost and unsaved. So, becoming a licensed Evangelist, I did not want to do this just to incur a title. I could care less about the title if I am not honoring God wholeheartedly, then I release it all back to Him.

> *"Looking unto Jesus, the author and finisher of our faith, who for the joy that was set before Him endured the cross, despising the shame, and has sat down at the right hand of the throne of God."* (Hebrews 12:2, KJV)

There is no way I could be a counterfeit when God loves me so much that He sacrificed His son to save me. Not only that, but He also left the ninety-nine to come after the one, the one being me. Every time I dwell on how much He loves me, I die to my flesh again, and again, and again. Continually succumbing to His will for my life. I had previously avoided the call of ministry for many years as my maturity level just wasn't there. I didn't think I was worthy or qualified, and then I realized the only approval I need is from God, it is He who decided that I met the qualifications.

"And he said unto me, my grace is sufficient for thee: for my strength is made perfect in weakness." (2 Corinthians 12:9, KJV)

But first, the breakthrough needed to erupt. Every hidden part of me needed to be healed. This was going to be an arduous process because all I knew was fighting. It wasn't that I liked to fight, nor did I want too. There were unavoidable occurrences where I had no choice.

I was surrounded by domestic abuse experienced by several women in my family. It became so disturbing to me that by the time I was fourteen years old, I helped my mother, my sister, and that spilled over into my own marriage.

I honor God too much to put on a performance. I could not put on a façade and pretend while remaining the same internally. No transfiguration was occurring. I was merely existing, which was my coping mechanism. Misplaced I was doing the same ole song and dance. But I had performed long enough, by going to church and then the local bar for $2.00 drinks immediately after service, becoming a drunkard which is a sin against God. I had the audacity to do this for many years, but now enough was enough. I had to change the trajectory of my life. The creator of everything, I owed Him my Life.

I craved the presence of God, a continual encounter with my Father. I had to draw closer to the Holy Spirit. His word says if

I draw closer to Him, then He will draw closer to me. I yearned to accomplish this. I no longer wanted to walk in the spirit of doublemindedness.

I desired to give God my heart, my mind, my soul. Intentionality was mandatory. Abiding in the Holy Spirit is where I always want to be. It is where I need to be. I am not even worthy of being loved to this magnitude but despite all that I've done that was not of God, He still loves me unconditionally. How could I not want to abide in the Holy Spirit. It wasn't always this way, as I hadn't always grasped what this entailed. I would just attend church and for the duration of the service, if I can be completely honest, I would feel entertained, just watching. Once service was over, I would leave the same way I entered. And for years I thought I was living for God. It is so much more to it, than just attending church, listening to worship music, reading the Bible, I could do all of that but if my intentions were not pure, then it was all in vain. How was my heart posture? I had to check the temperature of my heart. I no longer wanted to straddle the fence or be lukewarm, but I did everything to have God in the center of it all.

I was not fooling God. He knows all, and he sees all, which is why I'm perplexed as to why many are comfortable putting on a performance as if he only sees parts of our lives. We are too complacent with justifying our immoral behaviors.

Treating God as if he is a genie in a bottle, or trying to negotiate bargain basement deals with him as if he's a coupon God. How many times have your prayed for something, but you didn't even believe the prayer as you spoke it, you didn't believe that you were worthy of what you prayed for. I have personally done this numerous. times. I would pray and before I finished, I would say, "I know my prayers won't be answered". I felt as if my behavior wasn't deserving of all the blessings God had for me. God is the creator of ALL the universe and here I was compromising my faith. He is a limitless God who desires our love unconditionally. I fail God daily and He still loves me, how can I not submit to a love so pure and divine. I have been more committed to humans and worldly things.

We think what our heart desires is unattainable, but the truth is, all you need to do is believe and have faith and your intentions must be pure. I desired to *grow through life* and not just *go through life*. I needed to be intentional with every move I made. To do things just to say you did it, with no objective or meaning behind it, was just merely being. I wanted a life of substance, a life that had depth. I did not want to just exist. I knew that would transpire through pursuing a relationship with God, the Father, the Son and the Holy Spirit. I wanted intimate worship with the creator. And I wanted it to be genuine, not out of obligation as to receive something in return. I wanted to wear God like a garment. I remember hearing my Apostle Kimberly McClinton say that and it just did something to me. That statement was powerful. I wanted to Abide in God while being intentional.

Apostle Crishanda Burgos and Prophetess Deborah Anthony became a circle of individuals who covered me well. I had never experienced this level of covering and I am so grateful for God sending these women in my life.

One evening, my granddaughter, Bella Skye who is currently four years old, was at my house for the weekend. It was time for her bath in preparation for bed. And she said "Grandma, can I take my bath tomorrow"? I replied, "No sweetie, you must take your bath tonight". She laughed and playfully said, "tomorrow, tomorrow, tomorrow, tomorrow" and it just cracked her up. Suddenly the Holy Spirit reminded me of how I always said I'll do it tomorrow. My heart sank, because it was so true. I was notorious for putting things off until the next day, and then repeating the cycle continuously. I wasn't abiding nor obeying, I was being self-centered and focusing only on what I wanted, and not what I needed. I was focused on my selfish wants, and I wasn't focused on my purpose, what God ordained for me. I wanted my heart pure and on fire for God, but my character was dishonorable. We must appreciate the sacredness of God's presence. We must surrender daily and reverence our Father's divine provision. We must abort seeking worldly declarations, fulfillment in temporal things. Renewing of the mind and restoration is a journey to becoming healed and whole. When we do this then we are leading with intentionality and become Graced to Govern God's people well.

When I found me, and gave birth to my She Found Her, a Healed and Whole Soul Ministry.

> *"Give me an understanding heart so that I can govern your people well and know the difference between right and wrong. For whom by himself can govern this great people of yours?"* (1 King 3:9, NLT)

SUFFER WELL.

Mrs. Tracie Vick is a Licensed Evangelist, a published author of *Rewritten: I Am Free, No Longer Bound* and Certified Life Coach, deemed "The Turnaround Coach." She is the founder of She Found Her, A Healed And Whole Soul, DLM Legendary Consultants, LLC continuing her mission to help others heal and thrive.

FAMILY AND RELATIONSHIP

4

GRACED TO FOLLOW GOD

If You Do It God's Way, You Get God's Results

Drs. Hiram and Joronda Crawford

"The God of Israel said, The Rock of Israel spoke to me: He who rules over men must be just, Ruling in the fear of God." (2 Samuel 23:3, NKJV)

God will place you in a place of leadership and governance if He knows that He can trust you to follow His way and thereby get His results. God's results lead to blessing, expansion, promotion, and many other positive things—but not without challenges. The challenges are there not to discourage you, but to test your faith - you must press on. The interesting thing is that as you seek Him to lead and don't get discouraged, He leads and blesses. Then people give you the credit for how wonderfully things go. You MUST immediately throw this credit back to Him. God's way in leadership leads to God's phenomenal results.

Our Story

"Lead me in Your truth and teach me, For You are the God of my salvation; On You I wait all the day." (Psalm 25:5, NKJV)

The theme *"If you do it God's Way, you get God's Results"* has been the motto of our lives and has proven beneficial. As children, neither of us liked whippings, so we tried to do the right things to avoid them with our parents. We don't want whippings from God, so we live according to His precepts.

God blessed both of us with successful careers—Dr. Hiram as a professor and the head of his department, and Dr. Joronda as a teacher and principal. Neither of us sought out leadership, but it sought us out. The department recruited Dr. Hiram. One of Dr. Joronda's graduate professors said, "If you like affecting thirty children, what about impacting thirty times thirty?" That intrigued her. And so, our leadership saga began.

Concerning relationships, we both waited until marriage (remaining virgins) to have a sexual relationship. We both believed that God would send us the partner He wanted us to have or keep us single. I often said that I was so happy single to get married and be miserable. Because of these beliefs, neither of us was willing to get involved with anyone unless God had put His stamp of approval on that person. We knew that if the person was God's choice, we would have no problems loving them.

Dr. Joronda even broke off the relationship with Dr. Hiram. He had taken her out a couple of times. On this date, she asked him where this was going. When he couldn't answer, she said, "Well then, we need to stop seeing each other." He was shocked and complied.

After a few months, he knew where he wanted it to go and asked her out again. A godly friend told Dr. Joronda that she dreamed about a man asking her out just before Dr. Hiram did ask her for a date, so she knew that it was okay to proceed with it.

We offer more later about God using dreams.

Not Wanting to Miss God's Results

"Do not enter the path of the wicked, and do not walk in the way of evil. Avoid it, do not travel on it; Turn away from it and pass on." (Proverbs 4:14–15 KJV)

Joronda remembered, "Since we were in our thirties and forties when we got married, each of us was approached with temptations from other flawed partners. At one time, I thought that I would go into the mission field. A man who was over a mission organization proposed to me. I told him that I would pray about it. After prayer, the Lord said that there would be many false prophets. I wrote to him and told him no."

A woman approached Dr. Hiram. He had to leave her with his car just as Joseph left Potiphar's wife with his coat. Neither of us was willing to settle for anything but God's best. We knew if we followed God's way, we would get God's results. We also knew that Matthew's words were true.

> *"But seek first the kingdom of God and His righteousness, and all these things shall be added to you."* (Matthew 6:33, KJV)

And so, were those of Jeremiah 22:15: *"Shall you reign because you enclose yourself in cedar? Did not your father eat and drink, and do justice and righteousness? Then it was well with him." (NKJV)*

Receiving God's Best by Seeking God's Way

> *"And all these blessings shall come upon you and overtake you, because you obey the voice of the Lord your God."* (Deuteronomy 28:2 KJV)

Hiram's Moon Rocks

Hiram desired to go to the moon. He worked at both Argonne National Laboratory and Ames National Laboratory. Because he followed God's way, the Lord allowed the moon to come to him. He studied rocks that came from the moon.

Joronda's Mission

Joronda desired to be a missionary. Because she observed God's way, God allowed her to serve as a home missionary in many classrooms and as a school principal.

Bringing Them Together

"For You are my rock and my fortress; Therefore, for Your name's sake, lead me and guide me." (Psalm 31:3, KJV)

As mentioned earlier, a friend had a dream about us two. God gave Dr. Joronda a dream as well. She saw a table, a chair, and a sofa. She thought that this would be the setting in which he proposed. It turned out that it was a series of events.

They both knew a Mr. Bunton (now deceased). He was Dr. Hiram's choir instructor in high school and Dr. Joronda's all-city choir director. They mentioned that they were both going to his retirement celebration. They decided to go together. When they entered, Mr. Bunton said, "A marriage made in heaven." Dr. Hiram felt that Mr. Bunton was blowing his cover.

They then went and sat at the table that was in the first part of the dream. Dr. Hiram wanted to propose in a romantic place, so he drove Dr. Joronda to a park at the lakefront after dinner. The seat of the car was the second part of the dream. A police car drove up to them and said that the park was closed, so they would have to leave.

Dr. Hiram asked Dr. Joronda if she could go to his house because he had something to discuss with her. He knew this was unconventional, but she agreed to go. They sat on the couch in his living room—this was the third part of the dream.

Because Dr. Hiram thought Dr. Joronda would say no, he hemmed and hawed around the question. But at last, he asked her to marry him.

Joronda said, "Is this the question?" Dr. Hiram said, "Yes." "Well, if this is the question, then the answer is yes," she answered.

Dr. Hiram immediately called Joronda's father, Mr. Joseph Strong, to ask for her hand in marriage. Her mother, Dr. Dorothy Strong, was ecstatic. He then called his parents, Rev. Hiram Crawford, Sr. and Mrs. Eleanor Crawford. They were shocked and thrilled. Hiram and Joronda had a beautiful storybook wedding.

Preparing for Marriage

"Marriage is honorable among all, and the bed undefiled; but fornicators and adulterers God will judge." (Hebrews 13:4, NKJV)

Since they wanted to be sure that they were doing it God's way, they didn't merely go through a few sessions of marriage counseling offered by Pastor Hiram Crawford, Sr., Hiram's pastor. They also went through marriage counseling by Minister Herbert Porter, Joronda's then-pastor. They prayed and read a Christian marriage preparation book, *So You're Getting Married* by H. Norman Wright.

Hiram and Joronda went through a chapter each time they met, discussed its contents, and prayed about it. They later used this same book with other couples when counseling them. Each of the fourteen chapters of the book starts with the words "Commitment to..." and deals with every aspect of marriage. This instruction gave them a strong foundation for their upcoming marriage.

Finally, Minister Porter and Pastor Hiram Crawford, Sr., married them.

Standing for What God Stands For

"Watch, stand fast in the faith, be brave, be strong." (1 Corinthians 16:13, NKJV)

In doing it God's way, they knew they would have to stand for what God stands for and oppose what God opposes in their marriage, even when it wasn't popular. God created marriage between one man and one woman. God is also against killing babies in the womb for convenience's sake. We have stood with these principles.

Ministries

"Therefore, my beloved brethren, be steadfast, immovable, always abounding in the work of the Lord, knowing that your labor is not in vain in the Lord." (1 Corinthians 15:58, KJV)

Various ministries have been central to our married lives, and we have been active at our church in several capacities. We have also worked with our church's credit union, which opened in 1963.

Dr. Hiram is the President, and Dr. Joronda is the Vice President of the Pro-Life Pro-Family Coalition, which was started in 1985 by Hiram's father.

Early in our marriage, we started teaching a computer literacy class at Pacific Garden Mission—a homeless shelter founded in 1877 that has never closed.

After two years of marriage, we started counseling other pre-married and currently married couples. Dr. Hiram also worked closely with the Prayer Band Convention, which was launched in 1959.

In 2010, we co-founded, with others, the Faith-Based Credit Union Alliance, a 501(c)(3) organization that collaborates with 33 credit unions for support, networking, and training. In 2022, this organization received the coveted Herb Wegner Award from the National Credit Union Foundation.

Even vacations are a ministry to us. There is no vacation from God or His work. In each country we visit, we order "Our Daily Bread" in the languages of all the countries we visit, as well as in English. The people of these countries love the pamphlets we distribute. Many of them are learning English and prefer to receive one in English. Both of us try to support whoever needs our encouragement, including, but not limited to, family, church members, and others.

Caring for Our Parents

"Honor your father and your mother, that your days may be long upon the land which the Lord your God is giving you." (Exodus 20:12 KJV)

We believed that honoring and taking care of our parents was important and was God's way. As a result, we were caregivers for both of our mothers. Our father, Joseph Strong, stayed with us for a short time. It was a wonderful time of blessings and challenges. We enjoyed the Thursday Family Day when we took them out to eat. We have splendid memories and lessons on care from those days.

Your Turn – Your Challenge: Doing it God's Way and Getting God's Results

"But seek first the kingdom of God and His righteousness, and all these things shall be added to you." (Matthew 6:33, KJV)

You may ask, "How can I lead a fulfilled life complete with blessings and wonderful challenges?"

The scripture above has the key. The first step to salvation in Campus Crusade for Christ's "Four Spiritual Laws says. "God loves you and offers a wonderful plan for your life."

Because God, through His son Jesus, made you, he knows the ultimate best destiny for your life. Follow these steps to find out what that purpose is and thereby be fulfilled:

If you have not done so, Accept Jesus as your savior.

Pray and ask Jesus to come into your heart.

Repent of your sins.

Ask Jesus to direct your entire life.

Saturate yourself in God's Word, the Bible, starting with the book of John.

Have daily devotions in the morning before you start your day.

Find a good devotional to read, such as "Our Daily Bread."

Read it and the Bible consistently.

Pray about your day and ask God to bless it.

Pray about decisions and then obey what Jesus says.

Google states, "The average person makes 35,000 decisions a day." No wonder the Bible says in 1 Thessalonians 5:17, "*Pray without ceasing*" (KJV).

Obey and stand with God, no matter what.

See life's challenges as just that – challenges.

Challenges are not stop signs!

They are tests to see if you will trust God through it all. The children of Israel saw the giants when they were already in the zone of blessing.

If you know that this is God's will for you, forge on, and don't be discouraged.

Going on Your Life Adventure: Doing It God's Way and Getting God's Results

"The blessing of the Lord makes one rich, And He adds no sorrow with it." (Proverbs 10:22 NKJV)

We challenge you to move with God toward the marvelous destiny that He has for you. Step out in faith by doing it God's way and getting God's results. The places and positions where He will take you are frightening and challenging but marvelous. As my now-deceased college president, Dr. Robert A. Cook used to say, "Walk with the King today, and be a blessing!"

The song by Gloria Gaither and Willam J. Gaither keeps coming to my mind:

"Something beautiful, something good

All my confusion He understood

All I had to offer Him was brokenness and strife

But he made something beautiful of my life."

Drs. Hiram & Joronda Crawford - married for 33 years. Hiram, a retired computer science department chair; Joronda a retired principal. They co-direct the 40-year-old Pro-Life Pro-Family Coalition, an organization that teaches the importance of pro-life and building a strong biblical family in the black community. They are co-founders of the Faith-Based Credit Union Alliance, which services 33 credit unions nationwide. They have taught weekly computer classes for 30 years to homeless men and women at Pacific Garden Mission. They are board members of several organizations. Most importantly, they love Jesus and attribute all of their success to the Lord and His guidance.

5

GRACED FOR MARRIAGE

Governing Marriage and Family
Pastors Wesley and Neesha Stringfellow

Assignment

We got married in 1988—young, in love, and with a baby on the way, plus a 2-year-old son already in our lives. From the start, we knew God had a plan for us, even if we didn't fully understand it at the time. There were moments when life felt overwhelming, but we held onto one truth: God's grace was with us from day one.

Not everyone believed we would make it. People said we wouldn't last five years, and while their doubts could've discouraged us, they did the opposite. Those voices gave us the fuel to fight harder for our marriage and our family. We didn't fight to prove others wrong but to honor the assignment we felt God had given us—to build something strong, lasting, and rooted in Him.

It wasn't always easy. We faced challenges, made mistakes, and had to learn how to navigate life together. But through it all, we never let anything come between us. We chose to love each other daily, to forgive often, and to grow together. Most importantly, we trusted God's plan for our marriage and family, and His grace carried us through every season.

Looking back, we realize that understanding our assignment was about more than just staying together. It was about building a foundation that would leave a legacy of love, faith, and strength for our children and the generations to come. Following are some of the things we learned and now share with countless couples across the United States and abroad.

Practical Steps for Marriages and Families

Whether you're just starting out or have been married for years, here are some steps we've learned along the way to help strengthen your marriage and family:

1. Put God at the Center

    Make prayer a regular part of your relationship—pray together and for each other. Spend time in God's Word as a couple or family. It sets the foundation for everything else. Trust that God has a plan for your marriage and family, even when things feel uncertain. Scripture to Meditate On:

"Unless the Lord builds the house, the builders labor in vain." (Psalm 127:1, KJV)

2. Commit to Each Other Daily

    Treat each day as an opportunity to choose and give love, respect, and kindness. Never take your spouse or family for granted. Show appreciation regularly. Be intentional about spending quality time together, even during busy seasons. Practical Tip: Schedule regular date nights or family days to reconnect and make memories.

3. Learn to Communicate with Grace

    Be honest and open, but also listen with empathy and understanding. Avoid letting anger linger—address issues calmly and forgive quickly. Create a safe space where everyone feels heard and valued. Scripture to Remember: *"Be kind and compassionate to one another, forgiving each other, just as in Christ God forgave you."* (Ephesians 4:32, NIV)

4. Build a Community of Support

    Surround yourselves with people who encourage your marriage and faith. Invest in relationships that uplift and challenge you in a positive way—what we call FRAMILY (friends who become family). Don't be afraid to seek mentorship or counseling when needed. Practical Tip: Join a small group at church or start one for couples and families.

5. Define Your Family's Purpose

    Ask God to show you His vision for your marriage and family. Set goals together—spiritually, relationally, and even financially. Work as a team to live out the unique purpose God has for your household. Reflection Question: What legacy do you want to leave for your children and the generations after them?

6. Never Stop Growing Together

Embrace challenges as opportunities to grow closer to God and each other. Read books, attend conferences, or take classes that strengthen your marriage. Be patient with each other's growth.

The Value of Community

Early on, we learned an important truth: we couldn't do this alone. Relationships—true, God-centered relationships—were essential. We needed people who would stand with us, pray with us, and grow with us. This sense of community wasn't just about family by blood; it was about creating a family of friends, what we call FRAMILY.

FRAMILY is built on mutual love, service, and purpose. It's about asking, "Why did God bring this person into my life? How can I serve them? What can I learn from them?" Relationships shouldn't be one-sided; they should reflect the heart of God—full of grace, forgiveness, and understanding.

Grace in Every Relationship

Relationships are never perfect. There will always be misunderstandings, hurt, and times when forgiveness is hard. But God has given us the grace to love deeply, to forgive freely, and to define the purpose of every relationship in our lives. We believe that if God has brought someone into your life, there's a divine reason for it. Whether it's to sharpen you, encourage you, or teach you something, every relationship has value.

A Legacy of Generational Blessing

As we reflect on the promise God gave to Abraham, we see that His blessings extend through generations. Galatians 3:29 reminds us, *"If you belong to Christ, then you are Abraham's seed, and heirs according to the promise"* (NIV). This blessing isn't just about material prosperity; it's about the relationships and legacy we leave behind.

Our prayer has always been to build a strong marriage and family that honors God and to extend that same grace to others. Through FRAMILY, we aim to create a community where marriages are strong, families stay connected, and friends become like family. We are heirs to the generational blessing of Abraham, and it's our responsibility to steward it well.

Marriage: A Covenant of Grace

The covenant of marriage is not just for companionship but for the manifestation of God's purpose on earth. Through marriage, God establishes families that carry His generational blessing. In Genesis 12:2-3, God promises Abraham, *"I will make you into a great nation, and I will bless you; I will make your name great, and you will be a blessing. I will bless those who bless you, and whoever curses you I will curse; and all peoples on earth will be blessed through you"* (NIV). This blessing flows through marriage and family, as it becomes the channel for raising godly generations.

Grace to Govern Through Love and Submission

Governance in marriage begins with understanding the roles ordained by God. Ephesians 5:22-25 provides a framework:

> *"Wives, submit yourselves to your own husbands as you do to the Lord. Husbands, love your wives, just as Christ loved the church and gave himself up for her."* (NIV)

Submission and love are not acts of domination or passive compliance; they are acts of grace. A wife's submission mirrors her trust in God's plan, while a husband's love reflects Christ's sacrificial care. This mutual grace creates a foundation for peace, understanding, and divine alignment in marriage.

Generational Blessings Through Godly Parenting

God's grace empowers parents to:

Teach His Word (Deuteronomy 6:6-7).

Model godly character (Titus 2:7-8).

Discipline with love (Hebrews 12:6).

When parents govern their households with grace, they establish a legacy of faith, ensuring that the promises made to Abraham continue through the seed of faith.

> *"Blessed are those who fear the Lord, who find great delight in his commands. Their children will be mighty in the land; the generation of the upright will be blessed."* (Psalm 112:1-2 NIV)

Many years ago, our family embraced Family Prayer, we all gathered to pray and encourage one another. This brought our families closer, as we began to grow our families became a testament to God's faithfulness. They began to demonstrate the reality of His promises to Abraham and reflect His kingdom on earth.

God has given us the grace to govern marriage and family as a sacred trust. Through love, submission, prayer, and the Word, we can steward these relationships for His glory. The promise of generational blessing, rooted in the seed of Abraham, is ours to claim as we walk in faith and obedience. It is our assignment to govern our marriages and families with the grace that flows from God's throne, ensuring that His purposes are fulfilled through us and in the generations to come.

Encouragement for Others

Marriage and family are divine institutions established by God to be governed with wisdom, love, and grace. They are not merely social constructs but spiritual assignments that reflect God's kingdom on earth. As believers, we are given the grace to govern our marriages and families according to God's design, ensuring that His promises to Abraham and his descendants are realized through generational blessings.

To our family, our children and grandchildren, to every couple, every family, and every individual reading this: God's grace is sufficient. Whether you're navigating the challenges of marriage, raising a family, or building relationships in your community, His grace will sustain you. Love deeply. Forgive often. Seek the purpose in every connection. And remember, you are part of a greater legacy—the seed of Abraham, covered by the blood of Jesus Christ.

Get connected with a community that will stretch you, support you and challenge you to be a better you. It is a vital part of growth in your life and in all your relationships. Let's build together. Let's love intentionally. Let's govern our relationships with the grace God has freely given us.

A Final Word

Marriage and family are gifts, but they also take work. God's grace is always there to guide, sustain, and strengthen you. When life feels overwhelming, lean into Him. Choose each other daily, stay connected to your purpose, and remember—you're not in this alone. God is always working behind the scenes, building something beautiful in and through your relationship.

You've got this, and with God's grace, your marriage and family can thrive.

Wesley and Neesha Stringfellow, married for 36 years, are pastors, authors, and directors of HeartLife Ministries, dedicated to saving marriages and equipping couples with tools for enduring relationships. Certified counselors, they lead premarital and marriage programs, offering support through their books *Reboot Your Marriage and Masters of Marriage*. Neesha, an entrepreneur and founder of Neesha's Network, connects and empowers professionals while serving globally, inspiring couples to overcome challenges and embrace God's role in their marriage. Their impact is heartfelt and far-reaching.

6

GRACE TO PARENT

Look Into Their Eyes and See Their Heart
Dr. Alice Maria Crawford

I am the mother of eight children born through me. Having children does not make you an expert on raising children, however. Unless you confess it might make you an expert on what not to do in raising them.

No parents have a pre-planned agenda to follow when their children are born. Perhaps the best roadmap that young parents could hope for would be to look back on is the happy marriage of their respective parents. What if there is no happy home to look back on? What if there is no one that either parent can look to as a model parent? It is certain that we now have a generation where census statistics show that over eleven million children live in a single parent household. Eighty percent of that number is headed by a female, with twenty percent headed by a male. Does this diminish their odds to be a successful parent?

Reliable studies show the disparity between the educational attainment and income level of children who live in two-parent homes, as opposed to those who live in single parent homes, especially female-headed. Yet, even with all the advantages that a two-parent home can provide, there is no guarantee that these homes will produce healthy adults. The news is full of some of the most affluent parents who have children that have serious problems. Parents cannot give emotional stability and a healthy outlook on life if they do not possess those things. If the current parents did not see what "healthy" homes looked like, it will be difficult for them to be able to conjure that up. It also must be said that two healthy parents doing all they know to raise their children in a healthy environment can still have children who have serious issues.

Where Does That Put Our Children?

Where that puts the children of this generation can sometimes be at a very difficult place. According to the Center for Disease Control, statistics in 2020-21, there were increased percentages of children suffering from anxiety, depression, and behavioral problems. While we know that Covid was a big contributor, we also know that post-covid stats are not much better.

Children from the ages of six months to five years in most instances flourish. They are affectionate, they tend to bounce back even when things don't go their way, and they smile and laugh. Even children in homes that are dysfunctional – those children love their parent(s) and want very much to be loved by them. Why do children after this age show increased signs of emotional or mental disorder? There are a multitude of reasons, but one major factor lies in the disconnect they begin to experience with the adults in their life. By not receiving the emotional security that they need, they tend to build walls around their heart, walls that resist others.

Adults today tend to be less understanding of what is typical childhood behavior. Proverbs 22:15 says that: *"Foolishness is bound in the heart of a child ..."* (KJV). Children are prone to get into mischief. They are in their formative years and someone older and wiser must help those years be 'formed' into a good character.

I contend that despite the many changes that society has experienced, if you look into the eyes of a child, you will see their heart. You will see a heart crying out to be nurtured, to be loved, to be guided, and to have boundaries set for them. I would be the last to say that in looking into some children's eyes you won't see a cold, barren expression because that child has not experienced the love and affirmation of someone who would give them value. You can even look into some very young children's eyes and see that life has already jaded them to the point where they have no expectations of anything good happening in their life.

This is why it takes the Holy Spirit to show you beyond their physical eye to the eye of their soul, a soul that reflects their heart. Those of us who are believers know that God can take a stony heart and replace it with a heart of clay.

What Will It Take to Change a Generation That Has Never Experienced Unconditional Love?

It is going to take followers of Jesus who love His people and believe His word. It is going to take committed people who have a real desire to see the earth flooded with the gospel of Jesus Christ. It is going to take strong, valiant people who will not be offended by smart mouthed retorts from children whose hearts have been crushed. It's going to take disciples of Christ who have a determination to make other disciples, not as a social program, but as an eternal mandate to upbuild God's kingdom. It's certainly going to take those who know the power of prayer, who have faith that can move mountains, the experience of waiting on God, and the fortitude to move into the enemies' camp with full intent to tear his kingdom down!

And most of all it's going to take those who have the sensitivity to look into the eyes of a hurting child and see past their pain, into their heart which is crying out for love and affirmation. It will take those who have a grace to govern parenthood, even if you are not that parent.

Will you be that one?

CHURCH AND LEADERSHIP

7

GRACED FOR SUCCESS

Leadership Plus Team Plus Teamwork

Bishop Steven Jacobs

One of the first gifts that God gave to man was leadership—the authority to lead and govern the earth. After that, God gave man the gift of teamwork. It was God who said, *"It is not good that man should be alone; I will make him a helper comparable to him"* (Genesis 2:18, WEB).

God saw this partner would assist him in accomplishing His vision and mission on the earth. Both these graces flow from God. After all, when God got ready to create the earth, He said, *"Let us"* (Genesis 1:26, KJV).

I have learned that the greatest leaders understand that the power to success is released through teamwork, positioning the right people in the right place to do the right things. Great leaders see value in others, add value to others, and position themselves where they add the most value.

That is like Jesus' approach to leadership. As we hear from Paul in Ephesians 4:7, 8, 11, 12, 16 (NKJV):

> *"But to each one of us grace was given according to the measure of Christ's gift. Therefore, He says: 'When He ascended on high, He led captivity captive and gave gifts to men.' And He Himself gave some to be apostles, some prophets, some evangelists, and some pastors and teachers, for the equipping of the saints for the work of ministry, for the edifying of the body of Christ, from whom the whole body, joined and knit together by what every joint supplies, according to the effective working by which every part does its share, causes growth of the body for the edifying of itself in love."*

Jesus is not just building a church for us but also through us, with us, and of us. Every mission and every work in ministry needs leadership, a team, and teamwork to be successful. Jesus's process for building His Kingdom will always revolve around:

- Relationships
- Partnerships
- Leadership
- Discipleship

- Fellowship
- Workmanship
- Stewardship

Paul paints a clear picture of what it looks like above passage from Ephesians 4.

Leadership gifts are needed because there is a purpose and purpose needs partnerships to be accomplished and people must be prepared, positioned, and pointed in the right direction to accomplish the vision and mission. One of my mentors, John Maxwell, taught us "that leaders know the way, go the way, and show the way."

Though leadership is a key element of every vision and every team, it will serve us well to learn and maintain a mindset that no one of us is greater than all. Pursuing a purpose is not possible without partnerships; therefore, we will always be better together.

The need in a particular moment gives a gift priority and precedence. This mindset will eliminate jealousy, competition, comparison, and a superiority complex. It ensures the right attitudes and actions toward each other and the ministry.

In the kingdom of God, it is not about our role but about our function in the body. We can reach the highest levels of our potential when each of us has value added to us. Leaders, we must each understand the fivefold leadership gifts in the body of Christ and in our lives to equip us for our ministry work. We must understand the nature and purpose of our function, which is to pour or sow into those who serve with us/under us and to:

- prepare them for work in ministry.

- help mature them in the faith and doctrines of Christ so that they are not tossed to and fro by the trickery of men and never get settled into a local body because they are following human popularity and movements.
- grow up in all things into Christ and learn to speak the truth in love and learn to receive the truth spoken in love.
- be positioned together in unity with the whole body/team and not just your ministry or personal agenda.
- prepare and position others' gifts in the body where their gifts add value to every other member of the team/body. Prepare and position them to do their share to create growth, edifying, and nurturing of the body in love, not just the individual.

Leaders, when we ask people to serve on our team to help accomplish a God-given vision or purpose, we should not see them as someone who can make us great. When we position them in work on our team, they should become someone doing great things in the kingdom, adding value to the body of Christ.

Preparing and positioning them creates a runway for them to start sowing those seeds in the lives of others so they can be fruitful and multiply the fruit in them. By following Christ's original design, we will see them build something in and for the whole body/team. We will see them become someone who can add a specific value to a particular place in Christ's body and make the body/team great.

No matter our position in the body or our gifts, no one will ever be more me and uniquely me than me. Also, no other body members will be more uniquely them than them.

As we see in Romans 12:3–5 (NKJV):

> *"For I say, through the grace given to me, to everyone who is among you, not to think of himself more highly than he ought to think, but to think soberly, as God has dealt to each one a measure of faith. For as we have many members in one body, but all the members do not have the same function. So, we, being many, are one body in Christ, and individually members of one another."*

And Paul further validates this in 1 Corinthians 12:21 (NKJV):

> *"But now indeed there are many members, yet one body. And the eye cannot say to the hand, 'I have no need of you'; nor again the head to the feet, 'I have no need of you.'"*

We need each other's gifts, given by God, to mature, unify, and manifest Christ in the body. We should reject any teachings that deny the body of Christ or any Christ-given gifts.

According to this scripture, no body member has the authorization or the right to determine that another's gift is no longer needed or pertinent. We have been graced for success through the gifts of leadership, team, and teamwork.

The maximum potential of my gift and gifts of the body of Christ on this earth is not just locked in and released from a lone person; it is locked up and released from the whole body. God did not say to be fruitless: subtract and diminish, but rather, to be fruitful, multiply, and replenish the earth. The design of our gift is not about our greatness but the greatness, success, and effectiveness of the entire body that empowers us to accomplish Christ's vision and mission.

Systems of religion like to hold elections based on the popularity of established rulers and rank. The kingdom of God never holds elections; it educates, empowers, equips, and then appoints members to develop them in the body based on their Christ-given gifts. This is just like Peter, James, and John did with Paul and Barnabas.

As living stones or the building material that Christ is building His church with, we are all but humble believers who are being built up into Jesus Christ's spiritual house, which functions like Jesus on earth.

St. Paul tells us so in 1 Corinthians 12:27–30 (NKJV):

"Now you are the body of Christ, and members individually. And God has appointed these in the church: first apostles, second prophets, third teachers, after that miracle, then gifts of healings, helps, administrations, varieties of tongues. Are all apostles? Are all prophets? Are all teachers? Are all workers of miracles? Do all have gifts of healings? Do all speak with tongues? Do all interpret?"

Paul said, "*I am what I am by the grace of God*" (1 Corinthians 15:10, NTFE). Whether I am an apostle or have the gift of miracles, healing, help, administrations, or varieties of tongues, Christ has predetermined it.

It is not about my role but about fulfilling His goal, which is greater than mine. We are unique by divine design. Our gifts are different, so we cannot compete with one another but rather complete one another. Paul is very clearly telling us that we cannot allow the diversity in the body to divide or distance us from each other. We are unique by design because all of us are needed. The connection team waving and greeting on the road is just as important as the praise team waving and singing on the platform. The teachers teaching the children are just as crucial as those teaching the adults. The message from one preacher is just as valuable and essential to the body as another's.

Jesus did not just call His disciples to be apostles and release them to teach and preach the gospel of the kingdom. He personally picked them, poured and sowed Himself into them, and positioned them to repeat the process in the believers of the first church. Luke tells us in Acts 2 that these believers continued steadfastly in the doctrine of the apostles or their Christ-appointed leaders.

Through the equipping for a work in ministry through five-fold ministry gifts of the apostle, the prophet, the evangelist, pastor and teacher, these individuals with differing gifts in the body can mature, unify, and manifest Jesus on this earth so that the process can be passed on, repeated, and replenished to all generations.

Paul elaborates in 1 Corinthians 12:5–7 (NKJV):

"There are differences of ministries, but the same Lord. And there are diversities of activities, but it is the same God who works all in all. But the manifestation of the Spirit is given to each one for the profit of all."

Christ founded the church to profit every local body of believers in every community and generation. It is not about each generation or each ministry competing with and building up its ministry; it is about each gift edifying, complementing, and building and growing the body to a greater level of effectiveness, maturity, and unity.

I may have the gift of being a preacher, apostle, and teacher, but it is not just about me pouring out and sowing into others. It is also about those other body members using their gifts to sow into and add value to me.

> As we can read in 1 Peter 4:10 (NKJV): *"As each one has received a gift, minister it to one another, as good stewards of the manifold grace of God."*

Good stewardship is more than showing up to serve and pouring out what God has gifted me. It is also about having others minister to me from the gifts that are within each of them. The key to adding value to your gift is first having value added to it from a vetted and qualified gift of Christ to the body.

> Paul said it best in 1 Corinthians 3:6-8 (KJV): *"I planted, Apollos watered; but God gives the increase."*

Following and being positioned by a leader qualifies me to teach because I have first been taught. There are some folks in this body who, by Christ's grace, are doing great things in the greatness of their gift and going to go to the next level. Your ceiling will become your floor when you commit to consistently show up and allow other gifted people in this body to supply you. Christ has put a unique greatness in them, too.

Being taught is more than just listening; it is about being engaged, listening, learning, and then living it. When a thing is learned and practiced, it can be taught. We cannot give what we do not have or teach something we do not know. Once I have been poured into, prepared, and positioned, I can teach and give what I know and have.

Jesus entirely built His church for us and has placed the seed, water, and fertilizer in others so that they can sow into us, and God can give an increase. Jesus has given us a specific value and created a lane for us to function in the body of Christ. He unlocks and unleashes that specific value at its maximum in others. It is very important that we are committed and consistent in getting in the room with the other gifts of the body that hold the keys to unlocking and unleashing some kingdom assets and resources into our lives!

My goal is to evoke every gift in every person so that they are equipped for ministry, mature, and becoming unified with the rest of the body. Excellent leadership, great teams, and great teamwork can realize our dreams. Jesus' goal is not just to take us to heaven but also to send us forth to the earth. We do not need to constantly gaze at the sky, trying to focus on what Jesus is doing in heaven and wondering when we will be going there; we should focus on leading people to go forth to the earth.

Now ask yourselves:

- What gifts have you or your leaders discovered in your life?
- Are you intentional, committed, and consistent in getting in the rooms with others?
- What leaders and mentors are speaking into your life?
- Is your heart's desire to be great individually or to make the team great?
- Are you focused on growing and going?

- Who are you adding value to?

Each of us are in a process of becoming who God made us to be. Perhaps the greatest starting point we can take to begin our journey to success is to recognize that there are no lone rangers. We need each other to grow, to endure the challenges of this life, and to enjoy the blessings that God bestows upon us. Together we have a mission to build God's Kingdom on earth- together we can do it!

Bishop Steven Jacobs

A husband, father, and grandfather, I live in Pembroke, North Carolina, where I have been serving in church leadership for thirty-eight years. I am the senior pastor of Mt Olive PH Church in Pembroke, and I serve as bishop of Legacy 360 Ministries, a ministry that credentials, equips, and mentors pastors and ministers.

8

GRACED TO LEAD

"Remember You Are the Leader"
Minister Miyoshi Knox

When I first entered leadership, I believed it was all about getting things done by the book, with no exceptions. I leaned heavily into task-oriented practices, assuming that was what defined effective leadership. I thought if I set the rules and everyone followed, then we would succeed.

One pivotal moment in my leadership journey came when New Leaders for New Schools, the highly selective national preparation program for school principals, accepted me.

The program accepted only twenty-three Chicago applicants out of 400, and I was one of them. The program included six weeks of intensive preparation at Boston University and a year as a resident principal. Completing it earned me a master's degree in organizational leadership and a commitment to lead in an inner-city school for three to five years.

Sitting in a room of accomplished peers sharing their prestigious backgrounds, I felt insecure. Unlike many, I had graduated from Chicago State, an inner-city university, taking six years to earn my degree while raising a family. I worried they would judge me, and I second-guessed whether I truly belonged. When it was my turn to introduce myself, I spoke quickly, trying to appear confident while internally questioning my place among them.

Despite those feelings, my time at Boston University proved transformative. I learned under Dr. Gwen Lee, an exceptional coach who embodied Black Excellence and inspired us to lead with strength and vision. She taught me the importance of being polished, purposeful, and supportive of my team. I admired her immensely, yet my leadership coach shifted to Ellen Reiter when I became a principal.

Ellen was a petite, no-nonsense retired principal known as one of Chicago's finest. She had an uncanny ability to spot the strengths and weaknesses of her coachees. Early on, she coined my leadership mantra: "Remember, you are the leader."

Initially, I thought her phrase was meant to toughen me, especially after a colleague in Boston jokingly said, "You'll give all the kids another chance—they'll be hanging from the ceiling fan, and you'll still say, 'Oh, give them another chance!'" The room laughed, but I felt uneasy, questioning whether my compassionate nature was a liability in leadership.

early days, I tried to emulate others—becoming task-... and suppressing my natural tendencies. I wanted to show ... like Dr. Lee—polished and powerful—but Ellen saw right through me. During one visit, she asked, "Where is Miyoshi?" That question hit me hard. In trying to prove myself, I had lost the core of who I was. I had become—by constantly asserting my authority—a leader who questioned why a team member needed a personal day and even one who reprimanded staff harshly.

Ellen wasn't trying to turn me into her or anyone else—she wanted me to lead authentically as myself. That realization changed everything. I learned leadership isn't about a title or authority; it's about influence. Actual influence comes from fostering trust, showing empathy, and embracing the unique qualities you bring to the role. Ellen's reminder—"Remember, you are the leader"—wasn't just about authority. It was about owning my identity as a leader and showing up fully, without apology or pretense.

To leaders stepping into new roles—or those rediscovering themselves—leadership begins with self-awareness and authenticity. Don't try to fit into someone else's mold. Embrace your strengths, acknowledge your weaknesses, and lead from a place of clarity and purpose. When you govern well from that foundation, you inspire others to show up as their best selves.

I realized I needed to make deliberate choices about how I showed up for myself and my team. Leadership requires continuous growth and intentional action. And as the leader, there are three things you must remember to do to lead well:

- Invest in yourself,
- Be open to feedback, and
- Lead with intentional empathy.

Invest in Yourself

For the first four years of my leadership, the yearly 5 Essentials survey results were a painful reminder of what wasn't working. The survey is 360-degree feedback tool with which staff evaluate leadership to determine if the school is on track for improvement. It consistently showed that we were only partially on track. It felt like an indictment of my leadership. Despite my tireless efforts and pouring countless hours into the work, we weren't making the kind of progress I had envisioned. I was working hard but needed to do the correct and essential work that would lead to success.

Year after year, I blamed everything but myself: the organization, my staff, and my director. But deep down, I felt like a failure. Every year, I wanted to quit.

Adding to the pressure, I was losing key staff members. One by one, my entire special education department left. My assistant principal, who had been with me since the beginning, went to start her school. I was left to rebuild but needed to figure out where to start.

Eventually, I had to face that I needed to change my practices. The weight of these challenges pushed me to a breaking point, but they also became the catalyst for transformation. I had a choice: stay stuck in blame and frustration or invest in rebuilding myself. I chose to rebuild.

I started by seeking opportunities to grow. I attended Deloitte's Courageous Principals Program, which taught me to use business chemistry to strengthen communication within my team. I enrolled in Kellogg's Team Building Summer Course, where I gained valuable insights on cultivating cohesive, high-performing teams.

...ed in book studies with my director, reading works ...dership on the Line, Staying Alive through the Dangers of ...ding* and Developing the Leader Within You** that challenged me to rethink my approach and refine my strategies.

But the investment wasn't just intellectual—it was personal. I decided to show up differently. I adopted a new look—a new hairstyle and clothes—and paired it with a new mindset. I returned to work with a renewed sense of purpose, a fresh theme for the year, and a new love for the job. These outward changes reflected my inner transformation. I had reclaimed my identity as a leader, and that confidence became contagious. My team noticed, which created momentum that led to positive outcomes I had only dreamed of before.

What did investing in myself mean? It meant I stopped waiting for someone else to affirm me and took responsibility for my growth. It meant I showed up as the best version of myself—not to prove anything to anyone---but to lead in a way that felt true to me.

Be Open to Feedback

One of my most pivotal shifts was allowing myself to be vulnerable, especially with those who evaluated me. For years, I struggled to show my weaknesses to my director of school leadership, who also happened to be a dear friend. I wanted her to see me in the best light, to view me as competent. That need for validation made me hold back. I avoided telling her where I was struggling, afraid that admitting my limitations would make me seem less worthy of my position.

However, hiding my struggles left me feeling isolated and exhausted. I finally reached a point where I realized that I couldn't grow if I didn't let others see the real me. I began sharing honestly with my director where I needed guidance. To my surprise, her feedback didn't diminish me—it empowered me. She didn't see my openness as a weakness but as a willingness to grow.

That shift, though uncomfortable at first, transformed how I saw feedback. I began seeking it out from my director and my team. I conducted anonymous surveys throughout the year to understand how my leadership impacted my staff. The first time I read through their responses, I felt a mix of emotions—relief at the positive feedback and discomfort at the areas where I fell short.

I remember one comment, "Sometimes it feels like Miyoshi is focused more on the big picture than on what we're struggling with day-to-day."

That stung me because I thought I was attentive to their needs. Instead of dismissing the issue, I worked with a consultant to create a plan to address their feedback. Listening became one of my most excellent tools for growth.

What did vulnerability teach me? That leadership is about more than proving you have it all together. It's about showing up authentically, owning your imperfections, and being willing to learn.

Lead with Intentional Empathy

When I finally embraced that "Miyoshi is the leader," I realized something important: empathy isn't a soft skill—it's a necessary skill.

Early in my leadership, I struggled to connect with the younger generation on my team. I wanted to lead well, but I only sometimes knew how to meet them where they were. It wasn't natural for me, so I created reminders for myself. I kept notes in front of my desk and behind their backs where only I could read them as they talked to me.

The notes said things like, "Treat them well;" "Leave them whole;" "Listen to their ideas;" "You don't know everything;" and "You need them."

These reminders helped me lean into my natural empathy. They reminded me to slow down, ask questions, and focus on connection over correction. Over time, I began to see my team respond differently. They shared more ideas. They approached me with greater confidence. And they stayed.

Connecting was also about showing them through action that I cared. I worked hard to ensure clear systems, consistent processes, and inclusive communication. I adopted an equity lens, focusing on giving each person what they needed to succeed, whether it was additional resources, clearer messaging, or one-on-one guidance. I came to see that my role as a leader was to ensure my team had what they needed to realize our vision.

What did empathy teach me? Empathy taught me to slow down and truly see the people I was leading—their challenges, strengths, aspirations, and even unspoken needs. It showed me that prioritizing connection over correction creates an environment where people feel safe enough to thrive.

Giving each person what they need to succeed could mean providing extra guidance to someone struggling, giving space to a team member with new ideas, or simply listening when someone needs to be heard. Empathy showed me that leadership isn't about me; it's about what I can give to my team so they can grow, succeed, and contribute their best.

Most importantly, empathy taught me the power of presence. Being fully present with my team—whether in a conversation, a meeting, or a moment of decision-making—reinforced that the team members mattered. When people feel valued, they don't just follow; they commit.

Challenges and Solutions

Even when you invest in yourself, stay open to feedback, and lead with intentional empathy, leadership will still bring its share of challenges. These principles are foundational but don't eliminate the obstacles that come with governing well. Instead, they prepare you to face those obstacles with resilience and clarity.

Challenges are not signs of failure; they're growth opportunities. They test our resolve, push us to innovate, and remind us why we do the work. Here are three common challenges you may encounter and ways to approach them:

Resistance to Change

Not all resistance is actual opposition; sometimes, it's rooted in a fear of loss. When you introduce change, team members may worry about losing familiar processes, routines, or even their sense of security. As leaders, we must understand and address these fears.

Take time to analyze your team's responses and identify what they might be afraid of losing. Frame your message to acknowledge these concerns and reduce perceived losses. Involve your team early; share the vision and invite their input. This approach fosters a sense of ownership and eases the transition.

Balancing Authority with Empowerment

Effective leaders empower rather than control. To foster a culture of shared responsibility, grant your team the autonomy to make decisions within clear boundaries. By offering autonomy, you create guardrails that align with your vision while allowing your team to innovate within those parameters. When team members understand the scope within which they have freedom, real innovation can happen, and they feel trusted to contribute meaningfully. This balance allows your authority to feel like a foundation, not a ceiling.

Maintaining Consistency

Consistency builds trust, and regular check-ins reinforce alignment with team goals. Check-ins can be verbal or written dialogues, surveys, or scheduled follow-ups. Use tools like calendars, alarms, and reminders to maintain regular follow-through, and engage administrative support to keep you on track.

High-powered leaders must rely on more than just memory; structured systems ensure they notice everything. Consistency isn't just for your team; it's also a form of support for you as a leader. When you stay consistent, your team learns they can depend on you, and that trust strengthens the entire organization.

Conclusion

Reflecting on my journey, I see how governing well has shaped my leadership and the legacy I leave. Through clarity, support, and encouragement, I've kept my people not by demanding loyalty but by creating a space where they feel valued and respected.

Leadership is about serving others and empowering them to thrive. Governing well establishes a lasting influence and a unified team purpose.

To the leaders stepping into new roles—or those rediscovering themselves—remember this: you are the leader. You have been called to this place for a reason, and there is power in leading authentically. Challenges will come, and they will test you. But embrace those challenges as opportunities to grow. Be bold in the face of resistance—balance authority with empowerment. And remain consistent in your actions and commitment to the people you lead.

You don't have to fit a mold to be effective. Bring your whole self to the table. Lead with empathy, inspire with vision, and hold yourself to the same standards you ask of your team. Remember, you are the leader. Lead in a way that encourages others to grow, and the legacy you create will be one of integrity, trust, and genuine connection. In doing so, you'll leave behind a team and a lasting impact that resonates well beyond your time in leadership.

Wishing you well on your leadership journey.

Leadership on the Line, Staying Alive through the Dangers of Leading. Ronald A. Heifetz and Marty Linksy.

**Developing the Leader within You 2.0.* John C. Maxwell

Both books listed, Leadership on the Line and Developing the Leader Within You 2.0, are invaluable resources that have not only guided my leadership journey but can also provide you with practical insights and strategies to grow as an effective leader.

Miyoshi Knox, an award-winning leader with over 23 years in education and higher ed, empowers leaders worldwide through her consulting firm, The Leadership Perspective. A sought-after speaker and coach, she specializes in leadership development, innovation, and change management, inspiring others with her passion for people and meaningful connections. A grateful mother of four adult sons and grandmother to 11 grandchildren, Miyoshi invites you to visit theleadershipperspective.com and schedule a leadership boost today.

9

GRACED FOR PURPOSE

When Purpose is Contrary to Promise
Apostle Michelle Kelly

"You are built for what you are supposed to do." God built you, designed you, and gave you the right makeup for your purpose. But what do you do when it seems like your purpose is contrary to God's promise? What do you do when it feels like the promise you've been waiting for is slipping through your fingers, and your purpose seems completely out of reach?

I've been there. I've asked God the hard questions when everything about my purpose seemed in contradiction to the promises He spoke over my life. But in those moments of confusion, one thing remains certain - everything about you is determined by your purpose. Just like Jeremiah, God knew you even before you were born. Your purpose was laid out for you long before your birth, and even though it may seem hard to grasp at times, you are built for exactly what God has called you to do.

Consider Jeremiah's story. When God called him, He told him, *"Before I formed thee in the belly I knew thee; and before thou camest forth out of the womb, I sanctified thee, and I ordained thee a prophet unto the nations"* (Jeremiah 1:5, KJV). Jeremiah's immediate response was one many of us have had when God calls us to something greater than we feel capable of: *"Ah, Lord God! behold, I cannot speak: for I am a child"* (Jeremiah, 1:6). Jeremiah felt inadequate. He felt too young, too inexperienced, and too unqualified. Yet, God responded, *"Say not, I am a child: for thou shalt go to all that I shall send thee, and whatsoever I command thee thou shalt speak"* (Jeremiah 1:7, KJV). In that moment, Jeremiah was reminded that his purpose was determined before his birth. God had already equipped him with everything he needed for the task ahead. Even though he couldn't see it yet, Jeremiah was built to be a prophet. His voice—what he believed to be a weakness—was, in fact, the very tool God would use to accomplish His purpose. Jeremiah was built for that purpose, just as you are built for yours.

There are moments in life when we doubt our calling, when our purpose seems impossible or contradictory to what we see in the natural. Yet, in the unseen and the unknown, God is at work, crafting us, shaping us, and refining us for the journey ahead. Just as God refined Jeremiah, He is refining you. Every gift, every talent, every experience you've had is part of the preparation for your purpose.

This brings me to an example I want to share—one from my own life. I have a spiritual daughter whom God called to be a pastor. She had heard the call clearly, but she struggled with accepting it because of the physical challenges she faced. She had a limp, and her face had been disfigured by sickness during her youth. Moreover, she was a woman, and in the culture, she grew up in, that seemed to be a disqualifier. She believed that her conditions, both physical and societal, would prevent her from fulfilling the call on her life.

I watched as she wrestled with this calling. I began to pour into her, reminding her that God had known every struggle she would face and that He still called her to fulfill her purpose. Just like Moses, who questioned his own ability due to his speech impediment, my daughter didn't realize that God had already equipped her with everything she needed to carry out His will. Her purpose wasn't despite her challenges — it was because of them. She was built for what she was called to do, and God would use everything in her to fulfill that purpose.

Purpose and Promise: A Divine Connection

When we think about purpose and promise, we often see them as separate entities. We think of purpose as the journey we must walk, and the promise as the destination we are striving for. But what if the two are interconnected in a way we've never considered? God doesn't give us a purpose without also giving us a promise, but the path to that promise often requires us to walk through seasons that challenge everything we believe about our purpose.

Take Abraham, for example. God told Abraham, "*As for me, behold, my covenant is with thee, and thou shalt be a father of many nations*" (Genesis 17:4, KJV). This was God's promise to Abraham. But Abraham had to walk through years of uncertainty, years of waiting, and years of disappointment before he saw the fulfillment of that promise. There were moments when Abraham's purpose seemed in direct contradiction to the promise.

In the waiting seasons, Abraham struggled with doubt. He and Sarah waited for decades for the child of promise. In the natural, it seemed impossible. Sarah was barren, and they were both advanced in age. But God's promise wasn't bound by their circumstances. In fact, God often allows us to reach the end of our own abilities, just as Abraham and Sarah did, so that when the promise is fulfilled, we know it was nothing short of divine intervention.

What do we do in those moments when our purpose seems at odds with the promise? We trust in the character of God. We trust that His promises are 'yes' and 'amen' (2 Corinthians 1:20, NIV). We trust that what God has spoken over our lives will come to pass, even when the path to fulfillment is unclear. God doesn't make promises He can't keep. What He says, He will do.

The Power of Divine Timing

This concept of purpose being contrary to promise can also be seen in Joseph's life. Joseph had a dream at a young age that he was destined to be in a place of authority, to rule over his brothers and even his family. But instead of walking straight into that position of power, Joseph found himself in a pit, then sold into slavery, and later imprisoned. Everything in his life seemed to take him further away from the promise God had given him. But Joseph's purpose was unfolding in those very detours.

Each trial Joseph faced was part of the divine timing that led him to his appointed place. His brothers' betrayal, his time in Potiphar's house, his imprisonment—all these experiences were necessary for Joseph to fulfill his purpose. And when the time came, God used Joseph to save not only Egypt but also his own family.

Just like Joseph, sometimes the detours in our lives are part of the preparation for the promise. In the middle of the storm, we may not understand what God is doing, but we can trust that He is working everything together for our good (Romans 8:28, KJV). The promise is coming, but we must first endure the process.

Grace for Purpose: Embracing the Process

As we walk in purpose, we must remember that we are graced for the journey. God doesn't call us without equipping us. We are graced for the process of becoming who He has destined us to be. The delays, the struggles, the detours—they are not signs of failure; they are signs of preparation. God is molding us, refining us, and building in us the character and strength needed to carry out His will.

But grace doesn't always look like we expect. It doesn't always come in a straight line, and it doesn't always come with ease. But grace is always present. In every season, God's grace sustains us and empowers us to continue moving forward, even when everything around us says stop.

When we feel like giving up, when our purpose seems contrary to the promise, we must hold on to the truth that God's grace is sufficient for us (2 Corinthians 12:9, KJV). We are built for this. We are built for the purpose He has ordained for us, and His promise will never fail.

So, what do you do when purpose seems contrary to promise? You trust God. You keep walking by faith, knowing that the promise is coming, and the purpose is being fulfilled. You were built for what you were called to do, and you are graced for the journey.

Apostle Michelle Kelly, a Jamaican native and founder of Truth Outreach Global Ministries, is a visionary leader, mentor, and kingdom builder. Ordained as an Apostle in 2004, she equips leaders, empowers ministries, and provides global outreach in countries including India, Haiti, and Kenya. A passionate deliverance minister, author, and teacher.

COMMUNITY AND SOCIETY

10

GRACED TO CARE

Amid the Fatherless and Motherless Generation
Pastors Jesus and Darcy Mateo

If you think the fatherless and motherless generation has nothing to do with you, you're seriously mistaken. Unfortunately, this is the perspective that many in the church and the body of Christ hold. It reflects a low level of concern, while God feels very differently about the situation.

If this weren't the case, there would be a foster care and widow ministry operating in the church you attend. The Word of God indicates that the fatherless and motherless generation should concern all those who claim to be Christians.

Let's break this down so that we are all on the same page. Psalm 68:5 states:

"A father of the fatherless, a defender of widows, Is God in His holy habitation." (NKJV)

This scripture shows that God protects the vulnerable, including children without parents. This underscores that God deeply cares about a generation lacking parental figures, and He calls on the people of God to do the same.

Shouldn't we want to mirror our King by taking care of what He clearly defines as pure religion?

As James 1:27 says:

"Pure and undefiled religion before God and the Father is this: to visit orphans and widows in their trouble, and to keep oneself unspotted from the world." (NKJV)

Here is a direct command from God to get involved.

Unfortunately, we see little emphasis of this within the body of Christ, unless we're talking about a soup kitchen or donating to impoverished children in Africa. While these efforts are important, we face a growing situation right here on our own soil that demands more than just soup and distant handouts.

It's the foster care system, where God's children are often misused and abused. Recent reports have highlighted troubling issues, such as unsaved caregivers trafficking foster children for sex. These children suffer from emotional wounds, trauma, identity crises, self-hatred, and feelings of abandonment. They even suffer death at the hands of abusive foster parents who are supposed to keep them safe.

Shouldn't the body of Christ be the answer to this epidemic? We are the answer! God has given us a mandate to oversee foster care in our region.

In 2018, God sent us clear instructions to get involved with foster care and to establish a ministry that would address the lack of kingdom influences in this area.

This is how and why we began (TPSM). We created this to raise awareness within the kingdom about foster care and to take responsibility for what we have allowed the world to manage for so long.

TPSM also serves those within the kingdom who want to do more than simply express sympathy for children who cannot help themselves. We provide guidance on how to become foster parents and assist individuals who have little experience working within the foster care system. We do this to ensure that children experience God's love.

We have built a community of like-minded individuals within our ministry who want to see the vision God has given us come to fruition. We have helped several families become foster parents and have been a source of resources for many families and the children they foster. We are currently rolling out programs within the ministry to support these efforts.

The book of Isaiah 1:17 (NKJV) shows us what it means to do good. God had been observing His people, and what He saw did not please Him.

"Learn to do good.

Seek justice,

Rebuke the oppressor.

Defend the fatherless,

Plead for the widow."

The people were keeping the rituals, the festivals, and certain traditions but they were full of wicked acts. This was a people that were supposed to be His but were not reflecting who He was. So, He sent His Prophet to deliver a word of God's displeasure and the impending judgment to come.

It is very possible that the people in Isaiah's day thought they were obedient since they did bring sacrifices and kept other traditions. The truth is that they did not esteem God properly.

We can all potentially slip into this mentality. The word "esteem" means to value properly the worth of something or someone. You can set the value of God high or low. You don't even have to say it outright, but your actions can say it all and show if He is truly Lord over your life.

Here are a couple of examples of this. The first one we all should be familiar with is when Jesus spoke about the love of money. You can find this in the book of Matthew 6:24, *"No one can serve two masters; for either he will hate the one and love the other, or else he will be loyal to the one and despise the other. You cannot serve God and mammon"* (NKJV).

He tells us that either we will hate the one and love the other, or we will hold to the one and despise the other.

The second is a sad example of this, the rich young ruler found in Matthew 19:16-30, *"A man came to Jesus and asked, 'What good thing must I do to receive eternal life?'* (NKJV)

"Jesus told him to keep the commandments, to which the young man replied that he had. Jesus then told him to sell his possessions and give to the poor. When the young man heard this, he went away sad, because he was very rich."

He chose his riches over God and, by doing so, gave up true riches. I believe many Christians today genuinely love the Lord and want to do His will. So, while you may not be minimizing God's voice, it's possible that you are not hearing God's heart. I think we can look at the Isaiah 1:17 scripture and see if our good matches up with what God is looking for.

It is likely that many can't envision how they can be of any help when it comes to the fatherless. I can tell you with certainty that you can make a major impact. The fatherless lack the natural source of stability, structure, and protection that every child needs. When this is missing, the child is left to the mercy of whoever happens to be available to fill that role.

The world we live in can be cruel. The scriptures say this in Matthew 7:13-14, *"Enter by the narrow gate; for wide is the gate and broad is the way that leads to destruction, and there are many who go in by it. Because narrow is the gate and difficult is the way which leads to life, and there are few who find it"* (NKJV).

This means that there are more who are godless than God-filled. These are the influences they must endure. They have no sense of stability because all they know is brokenness. They may not know where they will be from day to day.

We adopted a child that we fostered. When we first got her, she was troubled. Her natural mother had abandoned her; her natural father was already in prison. She had been to at least nine other foster homes before she came to us at age nine. Several schools had expelled her by then because of her behavior. This child was broken since the mother did not want her, and even a family that tried to keep her afterward rejected her.

Trauma is common for children in these circumstances. This little girl needed stability. That feeling that you get when you come home after a long day is not something that the fatherless experience. For many children in care, they come to expect being constantly moved from place to place.

For this child, as she realized that she wasn't going to be bounced around any longer, we started to see improvements in her behavior. Of course, what was also needed was structure. She needed to know what she was doing, when it was to be done, and even why it needed to be done.

This was a struggle at first, but after a time of consistency, we saw the fruit of the labor. Her sleep patterns began to normalize, she started to develop study habits, and her anxiety began to diminish.

Stability and structure contribute to feelings of safety. When a child feels safe, they can put their guard down; they can open and start on the journey to healing. This leads to their need for protection. All children need to be protected, but who is there to protect the fatherless? God is calling us to this.

The word of God doesn't explicitly address the motherless generation, but Isaiah 66:13 reassures us, *"As one whom his mother comforts, So I will comfort you; And you shall be comforted in Jerusalem"* (NKJV).

Along with providing comfort, God heals our hearts when our biological mothers are absent.

I never understood how vital a godly mother figure was until I lost my mother to leukemia. Her absence created a significant void in my heart and life. I had the privilege of caring for my mother until her last breath, and those moments meant the world to me.

Consider the enormous hole left in the hearts of children who are moved into foster care, often without experiencing closure with their mothers. Even in situations where children may not have known the extent of the abuse they suffered, they still loved their mothers. She was the person who cared for them longer than anyone else.

For children who enter foster care too young to form a relationship with their parents, the impact is still profound, though you may not recognize it readily. The children we have cared for have typically been old enough to know their mothers, so they are devastated to be separated from someone they love. Some sit by the window, crying for their mothers, waiting for their return. Others have told us that they pretend I am their mother to help mask their pain, while others act out until they can see their mothers again.

As a biological mother of two wonderful sons, my heart breaks for those who are motherless. My grandparents raised me, and they fostered children throughout my childhood. Because of my mother's instability, my older brother, older sister, and I were all placed with our grandparents as wards of the court, like many foster children. God already knew His plan for my life and what it would look like in the future, and He planted and nurtured seeds over the years that grew into the movement we offer now.

What an amazing God we serve!

I never anticipated that I would follow in my grandparents' footsteps and continue the life-changing parenting they provided. All I knew was that children needed stability and consistency to build trust. God wants His kingdom people to provide these things to those He's entrusted to our care.

Get Involved, People of God!

If you are interested in fostering a child or may want to know how you can help in other ways, please feel free to reach out to our ministry—we are just an email away. We understand that not everyone may be able to take a foster child into their home, but there are many ways to help, and we will guide you on how to do that.

If you are a ministry leader and would like to start a foster care ministry within your church, we would love to conduct a seminar to get you started. Simply email us at admin@tpsministry.org or visit our website at www.tpsministry.org to request more information.

Yours in Christ,

Pastors Jesus and Darcy Mateo

FOUNDERS OF THE PLANTED SEED MINISTRY

Pastors Jesus and Darcy Mateo, leaders at Ekklesia Worship Embassy and founders of The Planted Seed Ministry, advocate for vulnerable children and families. As foster and adoptive parents, they share faith-driven insights on fostering, inspiring the Church to bring healing, restoration, and Christ's love to a generation in need.

11

GRACED TO BUILD

Activating the Entrepreneur Within

Apostle Eleanor Miller Stewart

Has a parishioner ever shared with you a business idea that seemed to appear out of nowhere? Perhaps they've shared their dreams or aspirations without any financial backing or support system. Maybe they had a solid plan, business acumen, financial resources, and people power but were too anxious or uncertain about stewarding the gift God had given them.

Do you see? They might be entrepreneurs!

The inspiration to write this chapter came from my experiences, scriptural insights, discernment, and encounters in leadership positions. In this chapter, you will gain insight into how to be a relevant leader who encourages parishioners to think beyond the walls of ministry and navigate life as businesspersons. As leaders, we are charged to govern, encourage, teach, and nurture our parishioners. It is our duty to be equipped with knowledge and a mindset of free enterprise to activate the entrepreneur within. I hope to build your confidence and skill set in entrepreneurship through personal anecdotes, scriptural illustrations, and affirmations.

The DNA of Entrepreneurship

Attraction to entrepreneurship can stem from many things, the environments that nurture us—biologically, socially, psychologically, and geographically. These factors provide the framework for our identities. Prayers and prophetic utterances also influence us, sometimes even without our awareness.

Both my paternal and maternal ancestors were entrepreneurial. In addition, I engaged in some form of commercial pursuit as early as sixteen years old and continue well into my seventies. Today I am seventy-five years old and thriving in my entrepreneurial lifestyle. The desire to reach beyond the status quo and establish a business seemed like the natural path for me. It was what all my family did.

Early Beginnings

Entrepreneurship is woven into the fabric of our family, influencing each generation in unique ways. From my earliest memories, my parents had "side hustles" that often didn't align with their primary careers, but their creative ideas helped sustain our household.

I remember my parents' recounting stories about their years together living in Arkansas before moving to Chicago. They described how they made ends meet by renting rooms to boarders while my mother cooked meals as part of the accommodation. My parents left sharecropping and entrusted my older sister and me with our paternal grandparents while they started anew in Chicago. They made this sacrifice to pave the way for our future. We reunited with our parents when I was about four years old.

In our early experiences, we pick up habits and adapt to what surrounds us. This influences our thinking and choices. My earliest memories of witnessing entrepreneurship at home were what I later called "The Friday Night Market" held in our small one-bedroom apartment. During these nights, my mother sold pounds of butter that she cut and wrapped from a 100-pound block. Our bathtub became the holding tank for raw fish. My parents transformed our kitchen into a culinary hub for fried fish dinners, and my father hosted card games.

If the usual market didn't produce enough funds, they hosted events where guests paid entry fees based on creative themes. My mother also baked and sold miniature bundt cakes she called "love cakes" and retailed her high-end clothes. My father worked as a sanitation engineer for the City of Chicago while simultaneously operating his paving business, Deacon Eddie Miller & Sons Paving, Inc.

As if that were not enough, he accepted a full-time pastorship and founded the Sure-Way Missionary Baptist Church. He successfully navigated these roles until his retirement and continued pastoring and operating his business until he died.

Generational Influence

My paternal grandmother, Elnora, created herbal remedies, which she bartered for necessities. My maternal Great-uncle, German, owned and operated a home-based business that included a grocery store and a gas pump on his property. My maternal Great-aunt Maggie taught piano and voice lessons from her home.

Cousins and other relatives also embraced commercial side hustles. My cousin Betty and her husband established and operated a restaurant on the west side of Chicago. My relative, Curtis Jr., owned fish markets.

My siblings also carried the entrepreneurial torch. After graduating from Howard University, my older sister, Clovice, opened one of the few Black-owned pharmacies in the Detroit area with her then-husband. Later, she catered special events throughout Chicagoland and Detroit.

My brother, Eddie, collaborated with my father at the paving company and took ownership after our father's passing. My younger sister, Virginia, inherited our parents' creativity for making things happen. She has operated businesses, including a thrift store, a residential and commercial cleaning service, and a catering company.

Later Generations

My nephew Jonathan and his wife Kelli are authors and own a publishing company, The Collins Books. Their daughter, Eleanor, started a stationery business at the age of six.

Biblical Insights on Entrepreneurship

The biblical text of 2 Kings 4:1-7 (KJV) tells the story of the prophet Elisha and a widow whose husband's death left her in debt. She feared that her sons would be taken as slaves to repay it. Elisha's solution did not involve giving her money directly. Instead, he provided her with unconventional instructions that required faith and action.

He asked her, *"What do you have in your house?"*

She replied, *"Your servant has nothing there at all except a small jar of olive oil."*

Elisha then instructed her to borrow empty vessels from her neighbors and pour the oil into them. When she followed his instructions, the oil miraculously multiplied. She sold the oil, paid off her debts, and lived on the remainder.

This story highlights several key points:

1. Resourcefulness: The solution started with what she already had.
2. Community Engagement: Borrowing vessels involved her neighbors, fostering community support.
3. Faith and Obedience: She trusted the prophetic word and acted upon it.
4. Entrepreneurial Action: Selling the oil was a business endeavor that resolved her crisis.

As leaders, we can draw parallels from this narrative. Like Elisha, we may not have formal training in business, but we can encourage our parishioners to recognize and utilize their God-given resources and talents. We can guide them to seek support from their community, step out in faith, and take practical steps toward financial stability and purpose.

Application to Leadership and Governance

It's important for us as leaders to challenge, encourage, and propel those around us to reach their fullest potential. While we often focus on spiritual matters such as hope, joy, love, grief, and social justice, we sometimes overlook the importance of empowering our parishioners economically through commercial pursuits.

Often, leaders may hesitate to encourage entrepreneurship because they may:

- have a narrow focus on traditional spiritual topics without integrating practical life applications.
- underestimate parishioners' abilities to flourish in entrepreneurial endeavors.
- fear that encouraging business pursuits might lead to the love of money, overshadowing spiritual growth.

However, when approached correctly, entrepreneurship can fulfill God's purpose, promote stewardship, and advance the Kingdom by addressing economic disparities and fostering community development.

Leaders may face challenges. They may be:

- uncertain about how to guide parishioners in entrepreneurship.
- have limited access to tools or networks to support budding entrepreneurs.

- hesitant due to traditional views on wealth and commerce.

But there are solutions!

Leaders can:

- pursue educational opportunities about entrepreneurship to support others.
- connect with individuals and organizations that specialize in faith-based entrepreneurship.
- integrate biblical principles that promote ethical business practices and stewardship.

By embracing these solutions, leaders can confidently encourage and equip their parishioners to explore commercial ventures.

Call to Action

This list of affirmations can empower you in assisting parishioners to activate their innovative potential:

1. I am a vessel for God's vision, guiding my community to see themselves as creators in His Kingdom.

2. Every gift and talent given to the parishioners is a seed for them to sow in faith, yielding blessings for themselves and our community.

3. As a shepherd, I inspire my flock to dream boldly, knowing that entrepreneurship is not just a calling but a ministry to uplift families and strengthen the church.

4. It is my role to remind my people that they are more than enough. God has equipped them with all they need to succeed.

5. The legacy of our ancestors is one of resilience and creativity. I encourage entrepreneurship as a continuation of that legacy, empowering the next generation.

6. I stand as a model of faith and courage, encouraging my parishioners to step out on the waters of free enterprise with confidence.

7. Private enterprise allows my community to redefine wealth as more than financial but as service, dignity, and purpose in God's Kingdom.

8. I see purpose in every idea and impact in every purpose. My people are called to impact the world through business.

9. By fostering an enterprising spirit, I help break cycles of dependency and unlock the boundless resources God has placed within each person.

10. With God's guidance, I lead my parishioners to embrace risk as a pathway to growth, trusting that He orders their steps.

11. My church is not just a sanctuary but a launching pad for dreams, ideas, and businesses that uplift the community.

12. I empower my parishioners to pursue entrepreneurship, knowing that every success honors God who makes all things possible.

13. I celebrate each business endeavor as a testament to faith in action, a blessing that can transform lives and generations.

Conclusion

As leaders, we have the unique opportunity to inspire and activate the spirit of free enterprise within our communities. We can help our parishioners unlock their potential, fulfill their God-given purposes, and contribute meaningfully to the Kingdom of God.

Like Elisha, let's guide and empower others to take action. Let's encourage them to use their resources, engage with their communities, and trust in God's provision. In doing so, we not only enrich their lives but also strengthen our churches and communities.

Entrepreneurship is more than a business endeavor; it's a manifestation of creativity, stewardship, and faith in action. Let's commit to activating the entrepreneur within those we lead, guiding them toward a future filled with purpose and possibility.

Dr. Eleanor Miller Stewart serves as the Senior Pastor of Sure-Way M.B. Church, bringing over four decades of pastoral and administrative leadership to her ministry. A dynamic and multifaceted leader, Dr. Stewart is also a licensed therapist, the CEO of Inspired Word Counseling and Business Services LLC, and the president of the Pretty Black Woman's Association, NFP. She leverages her extensive knowledge and experience to bridge ministry and community outreach, impacting both the public and private sectors.

CHALLENGES AND GRIEF EMOTIONAL WELL-BEING

12

GRACED TO PIVOT

Prepare for Impact

Apostle Dr. Crishanda Burgos

Everything was moving so fast in my life. God blessed me to marry at thirty in May 2019. The next year, God commanded my husband and me to start a church.

I would never recommend this to anyone. However, who am I to tell God no? The church was thriving; people were being healed, set free, delivered, and trained to reign. My position was number two. I wasn't officially the assistant pastor and didn't like the term First Lady' but I definitely did the work. I was comfortable being in the background, not carrying the full load. I enjoyed making the Apostle's vision a reality.

We were building at a rapid pace. By January 2019, we were blessed with a building, finally, after years of moving around like nomads. My husband and a few faithful workers totally gutted the building day after day. There was nothing left but walls and concrete floors. I enjoyed seeing it all come together piece by piece. Remember, I was number two, so I didn't carry the load. However, I assisted here and there, and I loved it. God has a way of preparing you for the unknown. We live life daily, hoping to walk into our destiny. Go after everything God has for us. Be who he has ordained us to become.

The Bible declares in Psalms 37:23 (NKJV):

> *"The steps of a good man are ordered by the Lord, And He delights in his way."*

The problem is sometimes we think the steps are easy. That the God we serve will allow us to glide down that prepared path! We often forget scriptures like 2 Timothy 2:12 (NKJV):

> *"If we endure,*
> *We shall also reign with Him.*
> *If we deny Him,*
> *He also will deny us."*

And Isaiah 43:2 (NKJV):

> *"When you pass through the waters, I will be with you. And through the rivers, they shall not overflow you. When you walk through the fire, you shall not be burned, Nor shall the flame scorch you."*

This is often the part we tend to forget. We will pass through these areas. We won't stay there. What I didn't realize was God was preparing me to pivot. I didn't see it coming.

SELAH.

> Reflection Question: *Have you ever experienced a trial where you felt forsaken or left by God? How did you feel? What did you do?*

I thought a Thursday in May 2019 would be a normal day, but my husband started feeling unwell unexpectedly. We thought it was just a flu bug. So, we treated it as such.

On day three, a Sunday, I began to worry. His strength started to fail. It was our day for church. I wasn't prepared to take the service. However, I knew he couldn't. So, I asked the Holy Spirit what to speak on. He gave me the story of "Elisha who helps the Widow and her Son" in 2 Kings 4.

I preached that message like there was no tomorrow. It began to minister to me and the people. I came home and had to rush my husband to the hospital.

> Reflection Question: *Have you ever felt so anointed in one moment and so helpless in the next?*

For three days we were in that hospital, praying, waiting, asking, seeking. Then the news came that he didn't make it. My life stopped in that single moment.

Questions and emotions flooded my mind like a tsunami. The people who were beside me faded away. My hearing became distorted. I folded. I literally heard my own heartbeat.

> *Reflection Questions: As in the story when Jesus heals the paralytic at Bethesda Pool in John 5:2-9, do you see where you can be healed but can't move to get there?*

> *Have you ever faced a situation that at once crippled you or made time stand still? That made your entire life seem incomprehensible?*

Pivot from Two to One

After taking a day to just be, I had immediate decisions to make. God had pivoted my life.

Pivot means to completely change the way in which one does something. The way I led my life no longer existed in any aspect.

What do I do with this growing church my late husband and I built from the ground up? Where do I send these people? I need to move south and restart my life. I will send them to quality leaders, I thought.

These were daily questions that filled my head. I had only days to figure this out because Sunday was coming again. So, in all sincerity, I prayed this prayer to God: Father, I love you so much!

Like the great apostle Paul said, "*I finished the race*" (2 Timothy 4:7, NKJV).

We built a house for you for eight years Lord. You know this was my husband's vision, and it is complete. We ran the race. We finished the course.

Now, Lord, I thank you, so that I will now move south and live. As I paused, and before I could shout "amen!", the Lord abruptly interrupted me and said, I want you to build me a people. I want you to build me a house. I gave you what you wanted. Now give me what's mine. Start again.

I was flabbergasted. Was the Almighty asking me to transform and become number one? The new pastor of the church? The one in charge? The one with a vision? The one who would carry all the weight!

My late husband had just gutted our church building. Who would rebuild it? I don't know a thing about contracting. I wanted no part of it. I've seen how the church treated pastors; I grew up in the church. I saw how pastors gave their all, yet people could still disrespect and disregard their sacrifices.

As number two in our Church. I felt these effects from the number one. I worked from nine to five every day and still had to serve people. My finances would go to making up the difference when people didn't want to sow. I was tired!

I wrestled with this for months and finally gave in to God. *"I will build you a people and a house. The only requirement is that you are with me! I will not do this alone."*

> The Lord replied to me: *"I am with you, follow the cloud by day and the fire by night."*

SELAH.

Reflection question: *Has God ever required you to do something you knew you couldn't do? What was it? Did you complete it? If so, how?*

New Technologies for Your New Pivot

> As it is written in Zechariah 4:6-7: *"This is the word of the Lord to Zerubbabel: 'Not by might nor by power, but by My Spirit,' says the Lord of hosts. 'Who are you, O great mountain? Before Zerubbabel you shall become a plain! And he shall bring forth the capstone with shouts of 'Grace, grace to it!'"* (NKJV)

The children of Israel were exiting a seventy-year sentence of slavery in Babylon during this passage. God was equipping Zerubbabel to transition them into their next assignment. They were given the task of completing the Temple.

Nehemiah had rebuilt the wall of Jerusalem over fifty-six years before. Now, with the help of the High Priest Joshua and the Governor over Judah named Zerubbabel, they would rebuild God's house.

During this time, Prophet Zechariah was assigned to Israel. I believe God was trying to give them new ways to overcome the adversaries connected to this assignment.

He was giving them new technologies and weapons. We must understand when God turns us into new seasons. New wineskins come with new paradigms, technologies, and weapons. The Lord told Zerubbabel not by your power, not by your might, but by my spirit. The new technology was the person of the Holy Spirit.

GRACE!

Reflection Question: *Have you ever had to change quickly into a new life without warning? As you look back on this time in your life, can you see where God was preparing you beforehand?*

The Movement of Grace

I was shaken by the thought of being responsible for people and their spiritual lives. All the things I had seen over the years frightened me.

When the Lord told me He was with me, it took years for me to understand the workings of Christ in my leadership. Then He began to teach me a weapon called grace in my fifth year as a senior leader.

One great woman in the person of Apostle Thibeaux told me, "God uses grace to go to war with!" I was astounded, so I did some deep study on grace.

Grace in the Hebrew stands for the number five. The Hebrew word for the number five is chamesh. Chamesh occurs when God's spiritual world steps into our material world. It stands for the five fingers of God.

In other words, when we can't accomplish through our own strength, God energizes our efforts. Grace is not a Band-Aid to sin. Grace is a movement, a person. Grace is the Holy Spirit.

I began to look back and assess the last five years of my leadership. Grace was with me the entire time. Grace was moving through me. Grace was working for me. The Holy Spirit held me up and helped me to govern His people in a graceful way. The

Lord began to staff my life with people who were connected to my life's mission. We live life together.

In pivoting me from number two quickly to being number one, grace sustained me. I healed and allowed grace to take the lead. I followed a cloud by day and fire by night. The Lord gave me new technology, blueprints, language, insight, foresight, and hindsight. The movement of grace restored me.

Let's Pray: Father in the name of Jesus, I pray the spirit of grace over my friend. I thank you that they pivoted quickly through obedience and were encouraged to move forward.

I pray even in the unknown, they obey you at once. The sovereign King has them. I pray that even in their darkest moment, when they want to hide and shut down, that the Holy Spirit would shine light for them to see.

Father, I thank you, that they would shout grace. Grace in every situation and circumstance that hinders their growth and development. I activate the new weapons and technologies in their lives.

Lastly, I pray grace would pivot them to their next, and they, too, would learn to allow the Holy Spirit to govern them through grace.

I ask this in Jesus' Name. Amen. Now, go, be powerful!

Dr. Apostle Crishanda Burgos

A 21st century woman of God, Dr. Burgos' fulfills the assignments given to her by the Lord Jesus Christ. As an Educator in the School system for over 25+ years, Dr. Burgos recently embraced full-time entrepreneurship and launched Recharge: Educational Solutionists, LLC, an educational training for Ecclesiastical, Educational, and Corporate. Apostle Burgos is a prophetic deliverance minister, and focuses on training, personal counsel, and teaching the word of God as the Senior leader of The Life Church Outreach Ministries in Hammond, IN, where "We are EXCITED to "DO" Life with you!

13

GRACED TO EMBRACE PEACE

Peaceful Urgencies
Pastor Miriam McFarland

Nothing gives my life more meaning and fulfillment than serving others. I believe that is how Christ called His followers to live. In my experience, this has meant balancing the joys and peaceful moments in life with the unexpected urgencies-- big and small-- that upend my plans and require me to lean into the peace that only God can bring.

Small urgencies were a daily occurrence when my children were small. They used to argue over the simplest things, from whoever had the esteemed privilege of pressing the button in an elevator to who would sit shotgun on a five-minute ride to the store. They would race, shove, argue, and cry to get what they wanted.

"Mama, didn't you say it's my turn?"

"No, Mama, he always rides up front!"

"She's using my pencil!"

"NO, IT'S MINE!"

While those little moments may not be urgent for adults, to three little people who were 9, 11, and 13 at the time, nothing could be more urgent. I would be frustrated at how I'd have to slow down or completely stop what I was trying to accomplish to address issues that were, to me, petty and insignificant. It felt like they wanted to wreck my productivity and plans for the day over something like whose day it was to do dishes or who was putting whose feet on someone else's chair.

Those small urgencies, as exhausting and irritating as they were, at the time, pale compared to the ones that change life. These urgencies bring a flood of emotions so strongly that you're shocked to numbness, unable to feel anything. They challenge our faith and require us to go deeper in God, to find the kind of peace that surpasses all understanding.

Two words. "He's gone."

Far from a childish sibling argument that would pass as quickly as it came, the loss of my husband of thirty-four years left me breathless and brought me to my knees. Then, just as I had begun to regain strength from the numbness of his absence, within three months, my mother-in-love passed, too. Three months following that, my mother joined them both. It felt like dominoes of death were playing with my heart. Three people I adored, honored, and enjoyed serving for nearly half of my life had left me behind. Gone were the hugs, laughs, meals, and prayers I enjoyed with them. They were removed from my touch in an instant. And yet… even through the intense pain of their loss, I found there was still a calm inside me. I call it "peaceful urgency," and it has carried me through.

In his small book, *Prayer*, John White, a twentieth-century Christian author, wrote, "Deep is calling to deep." He asserts that God planted a longing in each of us to commune with Him and that the turmoil we feel in times of distress is our soul longing for the comfort and peace that only comes from an abiding relationship with Him.

I have found that to be true as I have walked through the urgencies in my life. Peace comes when I respond to His deep call. His peace puts every urgent matter into divine perspective. It becomes an invitation to lean in and listen to His still, small voice. Even in the most alarming situations, the stillness of His voice brings indescribable peace that calms the soul.

The sting of physical separation that I experienced when my husband passed was the most poignant crisis that I had ever suffered.

I was no stranger to death and grieving. I had miscarried a three-month-old fetus and had delivered to full term a stillborn baby boy. I buried my beloved father too, but losing my husband was different. This separation felt incomparable to all the others. My faith and peace were shaken at the core, yet I found that my foundation held firm. I was faced with a choice between going deeper to receive a greater level of His peace and staying anxious in my grief. Deep was calling me deeper. Deeper than I had ever been before. The peace I'd known before seemed superficial compared to the peace I was called to in this urgency. To get the reprieve I needed, I knew I would have to respond in faith to His deeper call.

What did that look like? It meant taking steps each day to grow past my comfort zone. It required being vulnerable with others and trusting God as He walked with me in the literal valley of the shadow of death. Death was an enemy that wanted to taunt me to doubt God's goodness and the peace that was already inside of me. He put it there.

While in the throes of grieving my mothers, there were times when answering God's deep call looked like singing a favorite song of theirs or reading one of their often-quoted verses from the Bible. Especially, Psalms 23:1, *"The Lord is my shepherd, I shall not want"* (KJV).

By meditating on that first verse for a while I could reflect on how blessed I was. Having one praying mama is priceless, and God blessed me with two. Two role models who demonstrated how to trust God when urgent matters arise. What an honor that was. It evoked a spirit of gratitude that took my focus off my pain and brought me to a place where peace prevails. It caused me to reflect on the goodness of God in my life. Their songs and favorite scriptures awakened the reality of God's faithfulness to me. He has always ensured that I have what I need and more.

At other times, God's deep call challenged me to share my story with others. But I didn't have the answers I needed to feel qualified to share anything, I thought. I had too many question marks in my mind. I found God was not avoiding my questions; He was using them to draw me deeper.

In the moments after my husband's passing, my heart was flooded with questions. "Will You use me to raise him like Lazarus, Lord?" I cried as I laid my hands on my husband's lifeless body with all the faith I could muster to believe he'd rise.

But when my husband did not awaken, I answered God's call to go deeper by asking the next question: "What do you want me to do in this painful place?"

God's answer was simple yet profound. "Do what I created you to do best, serve others." At first, that seemed like a cold and insensitive answer to someone who was hurting. But answering God's deepest calls means trusting in His sovereignty.

Even through the pain and uncertainty, I had to stand on my belief that God knows me. He made me, and He has uniquely equipped me to serve others in this unfamiliar place. Serving was God's medicine for me. He knew before I was born that I would need help to serve others through my pain, so he gifted me the privilege of being the daughter of Pastor Hiram Crawford Sr.

I grew up watching my dad serve people in ways that ignited the love of God inside them. In watching his example, I developed that same passion. Joy fills my heart when I can serve God's people and share His all-encompassing love. God called me to share my story with others and to trust in His plan to heal my broken heart as I walked in obedience to Him.

While I shared my story with others, I found that my attention shifted away from my pain to the needs of those I encountered. Doing so summoned God's peace in my life. As I encouraged others, I realized I was also encouraging myself. When we share our stories with others, we have an opportunity to be God's vessels of peace. He wants to use our stories of how His peace calmed a lifetime of urgencies. Let's be willing vessels.

There is no urgency that His deep call cannot calm. Our stories serve as proof of how profoundly He loves us and those He has called us to serve. Our "peaceful urgencies" can be an answer to prayer for others in our circle. The greater the urgency, the deeper the calling, and the more profound is the peace He provides.

What urgency are you faced with today? I challenge you to get quiet enough to hear below the surface where "Deep is calling to deep", where His peace will calm the cries of your soul.

Rory Vaden, CEO of Brand Builders, said in a podcast something that I've never forgotten:

> "You are most powerfully positioned to serve the person you once were."

That statement prompted me to examine the person I once was. Reflecting on my triumphs caused me to remember the trials that God had brought me through. It was an act of obedience for me to be vulnerable enough to share my story with others. I thought to myself, "Who would care about what I had come through?" All that seemed so insignificant, but God knows our stories before we do. He works things out for our good in ways that we cannot understand at the time.

Let me share a few instances of who I once was. I once was a PK (preacher's kid) who thought my parents were too strict. Sometimes, I would envy other PKs, who seemed to have much more freedom. When I was young my dad told me I was a leader. He wanted me to set a precedent and to be an example for others to follow. As a teenager, I felt this was entirely unfair. But as I matured, I learned to appreciate his discipline. It taught me humility and positioned me to be an effective servant-leader as an adult.

I was once a college student about to graduate with a Bachelor of Science degree in chemistry with no idea of what I would do with it. Then, one day, my physics professor, who sensed my anxiety, asked me how I spent my time when I was not studying or working.

I told him how I served as a chaplain in my dorm, and how I took time each Saturday at a low-income housing complex tutoring children. I also took them on field trips and assisted senior adults with their needs in that community.

He smiled at me and said, "It sounds like you are already doing what you were created to do; have you ever considered being a teacher?"

A light bulb came on; my eyes filled with tears as I praised God for using my professor to draw me deeper into His peace. I didn't have a job offer for a teaching position yet, but God's peace eased my urgency immediately. It calmed the anxiety of not knowing my future after college.

I was once a pastor's wife whose life revolved around serving my husband, my family, and my church. Each of these roles demands a lot. Sometimes I was so consumed in fulfilling those duties that I allowed them to drown out God's deep call to take better care of myself.

At times, my body was too depleted to serve anyone. But God is so patient and gracious. He used my family and others in the body of Christ to serve me when I couldn't serve them back. He taught me to lie down and rest in green pastures as my soul and body were restored.

I share that to encourage someone who needs RESToration; spirit, soul, and body. Sometimes faithful servants have difficulty allowing others to serve them, and that can be a hindrance to our spiritual growth. My prayer is that you will grasp how God has positioned you to serve. As you reflect on the person you once were, the triumphs and trials of your life, you will begin to see how powerfully positioned you are to serve those God has called you to. Don't be afraid to share your story.

As we learn to become the person God created us to be, urgent needs will come and go—big and small. But the peace we've been promised remains constant. Jesus told His followers in John 14:27, *"Peace I leave with you, my peace I give to you; not as the world gives do I give you. Let not your heart be troubled, neither let it be afraid"* (KJV).

Jesus is speaking to us in this passage. If we live in the peace that He has given us, we will recognize that no urgency can triumph over His peace. So, as crises arise, remember to respond to His deep call to us. Let's continue to go deeper where His peace forever abides.

Miriam C. McFarland is pastor of Renew Church in Baker, Louisiana. A Chicago native, she began ministry under her father, Pastor Hiram Crawford, and later served alongside her husband, Pastor Bennie B. McFarland. Passionate about prayer, community, and spreading God's Word, she finds joy in family, pastoring, music, and football.

14

GRACED TO LAND

This is Where I've Landed
Elder Chandra Lace

Like many African American little girls, I grew up without my father in my life. He and my mom separated when I was 6 years old. I didn't understand much about marriage, or what was going on in my parents' relationship at that age, I just knew that a part of me—one of the parts that I needed to navigate my life was missing.

My father was a pastor, a profound preacher, and teacher of God's Word. I've been told by many of my father's family members how much of an excellent student of the Bible he was. They would tell me things like, "Your Daddy was a walking Bible. He was the one whom most pastors would go to if they needed to find a scripture or understand what a passage in the Bible meant. He was a Bible scholar indeed." Then others would share with me, "Your father was well sought after when it came to preaching. People would come from all over to hear him speak." The more I would hear those stories as I got older the more it fascinated me to know that my father was somebody. I had a vague memory of hearing him preach as a child. But the biggest thing I did remember was how much he would engage and excite his listeners when it was time for him to "hoop and holla." Everyone would be on their feet encouraging and cheering him on. It was an exciting sight to see!

In 2008, he passed on from cancer. Between the time that he left our home when I was 6 years old and the time he left this earth, our acquaintance was nonexistent to very little. He would pop in and out of our home every so often to see my eight other siblings and me. He'd hang around for a bit then be on his way. By the time I was on my way to high school, I didn't remember seeing much of him at all. In 1994, my mom, my siblings, and I were the victims of a house fire. We lived in a third-floor apartment building. The fire started on the second floor and immediately spread throughout the entire building. My Mom, my siblings, and I were able to escape the fire by jumping out of windows, and some of us tumbled down the back porch stairs all the way to the bottom. It wasn't until we all gathered outside that we realized that one of our beloved sisters, my best friend, was missing. We later learned that she fainted on the back porch due to the smoke and died. She was 15 years old.

Life became extremely hard and confusing for me from that experience, but I endeavored to continue living. I found comfort and peace in writing poetry. It became spiritual medicine for me. It seemed that that was the only way that I was able to express myself. I felt as if no one understood my pain or what I was going through because my sister and I were so close, in age and in relationship. When she passed, she took a huge part of me with her, and it took me many years to get those parts of me back. I would write poems as if I was writing to her or writing to God just pouring out my heart to them. I wanted my sister to know that I planned to keep our promise that we made concerning taking care of my mom. I have and still am. And I wanted God to know that I was angry with Him. I was confused. I was hurt. I was lost. And I didn't know how I was going to make it through the rest of my life without my younger sister and best friend.

As a result of everything that was happening in my life at the time, I shut down. I built a wall so tall all around me so that no one could get in or reach me. I simply became someone who existed. I didn't know my purpose or what I was supposed to be doing with or in my life. One of the things that my mom instilled in me as a child was that God doesn't make mistakes and that everything happens for a reason. That concept was very hard for me to believe because I couldn't understand how a loving God would take away one of the people who meant the most to me in my life. Surely, this had to be a mistake! But once I allowed my anger towards God to fade away, I began to turn towards acceptance. I accepted the fact that my sister was never coming back. And I also had to accept the fact that there had to be a reason for what happened to my family and I in losing my sister.

After I came to grips with my new reality, I began to talk to God a lot more. I would steal away to different places so I could have some intimate time with the Father. Because there were so many of us in one apartment, it was hard to have any type of privacy. So, I began to use the bathroom as my safe haven. I would go into our bathroom and sit on the side of the tub or either let the toilet top down and sit on the top of the toilet and share with God what was on my heart. I would talk to Him as if He was sitting right in that bathroom with me. I would stay in there for as long as I could, or until someone knocked on the door needing to use it (smile). Some days I would emerge from our bathroom feeling light and free. But then there were times where I would come out feeling heavy in my heart because confusion would often try to overtake my thoughts and sometimes "it" would succeed.

I come from a musically inclined family. My father could sing, and mother can sing. Most of my siblings dabble with music in one form or another, me included. By my freshman year in college, I began to take an interest in rapping. My older brothers were very much into Hip Hop music so sometimes I would listen to what they listened to. It inspired me how those artists would use words to rhyme and create imagery while "flowing" to the cadence of a beat. One day I thought to myself, "I can do that." I'm thinking to myself, "I write poetry so it's essentially the same thing." So, I sat down to write my first rap song. I had no problem with creating stories or finding words to rhyme.

My problem was trying not to sound churchy. My rap would sound nothing like the cool rappers I'd hear on the radio or the ones I'd hear on the tapes that my brothers would play. My raps would literally sound like I was rapping a sermon for church, and I didn't like that. I wanted to write something people could "bob" their heads to and rap along with. I didn't want to sound like a preacher. But the more I wrote the more scripture and Bible stories would come out of me. I became frustrated. I thought to myself, "What if I used some cuss words and talk about what goes on in our 'hood, maybe that will make my rap sound cool?" So, I set out to write an explicit "hood" rap song.

I found a published rap song that had a really nice beat that I could write to and began writing. The words were not flowing as I thought they would. In fact, it was a bit challenging to try and find a word that rhymes with a cuss word. But I was determined to write my "hood" song that I kept at it until I had written at least one verse which consisted of 16 bars (four beats per measure) back in the day. After I had written that one verse, I became satisfied with the fact that I persevered. I rewound the song on the tape and began to rap to myself what I had written. It sounded horrible! Not only did I not sound like I was not used to saying those words, but I sounded like a hood school professor who failed miserably at rapping cuss words! With that, I became discouraged and gave up. Why did I become discouraged? I'm glad you asked.

My entire life I've been labeled as "the good child" or the one that most of my family and friends expected to succeed in life and make something of myself. I never really had a chance to be myself or even err without people being disappointed in me or surprised. I wanted to live on the edge and do something out of the ordinary; something that I knew was completely out of character for me and succeed at it. But I failed miserably, and I became discouraged. It was then that I had to come to terms with who I was (am)—someone who loves God…loves the Word of God…and who carries the love of God in my heart. There was no escaping it for me.

Now, this is not to say that I'm a saint (far from it). Or this is not to say that I've never done anything wrong (of course I have—I'm human). This is simply to say that while I was trying to be like other people and appeal to a crowd that I didn't fit in with, I was trying to deny who I was (am). If you refer to the beginning of my story, you'd see that I was born into this Christian life. I come from a God-fearing upbringing. Not only was my father a pastor and preacher but so was my paternal grandfather (my father's father) so I got it honest.

It wasn't always easy trying to walk with God at an early age. Some of my peers weren't the nicest or most courteous. I had to deal with ridicule, name calling, shaming, isolation, hatred, framing and just pure evil from family, friends, and church folks. I've learned that when people don't understand you, they would rather make you an enemy than to get to know you. And that's essentially what I had to deal with my entire life. Once I began to see that type of pattern from different people, I began to pray and ask God to show me how to love myself despite how others viewed me or how they perceived me. I didn't want other people's opinions of me to affect who I knew I was and who God called me to be. I even had a prophet to prophecy to me these words, "There are a host of people that don't like you…and with no defining reason why." I was thinking to myself, "Really? That's quite interesting." Yet, I didn't let it bother me.

I continued to *let my light so shine before men that others may see my good works and glorify God who's in heaven*. I cannot control what people say, think, feel, or do where I'm concerned. I can only control how I respond to them and so far, I believe I've done a wonderful job forgiving and turning the other cheek. I used to say that God has given me an overabundance of patience and peace because Lord knows it's only God who keeps me in perfect peace when the devil tries to create havoc and cause chaos in my life.

To conclude, I've learned that in life, we often find ourselves navigating through storms that challenge our faith, break our hearts, and leave us questioning God's purpose for our lives. But let me remind you of this truth: *"The Lord is close to the brokenhearted and saves the crushed in spirit"* (Psalm 34:18, NIV). Every trial, every loss, every heartache we endure is not without purpose. Just as Joseph endured betrayal, imprisonment, and suffering before rising to a position of authority to save many, so too we can trust that God is weaving our pain into a greater purpose.

When I reflect on my journey, I see the grace of God guiding me, even when I didn't understand it. Though I was frustrated, God was faithful. Though I felt abandoned, He was ever-present. The pain that once defined me became the soil where purpose grew. Today, I stand not as someone defined by my trials but as someone empowered by the grace of God to govern my life with strength, wisdom, and love.

To those of you who feel crushed under the weight of life's trials, remember this: God sees you. He has not forgotten you. His word declares, *"I know the plans I have for you, declares the Lord, plans to prosper you and not to harm you, plans to give you a hope and a future"* (Jeremiah 29:11, NIV). Trust Him to bring beauty from your ashes, to trade your mourning for joy, and to clothe you with garments of praise.

You may not understand why you're going through what you're going through but be encouraged—God's hand is with you. The same God who brought me through the fire, both literally and spiritually, is with you too. Allow Him to heal your broken places, shape your character, and reveal your divine purpose. You are graced to govern over every challenge, every setback, and every heartache, not because of your strength but because of His.

Stand firm, beloved. Walk in faith. Live with hope. And always remember, God's grace is sufficient, His power is perfect in our weakness, and His love never fails.

Elder Chama Lace is a visionary writer and artist who blends storytelling with emotional depth to create impactful works that inspire and captivate. Since launching her career in 1999, she has published bestselling books, songs, and stories, leaving an indelible mark and empowering others to unlock their creative potential. www.chamalace.com

15

GRACED TO ENDURE

Challenge Your Challenges
Alexis Rosa Lowry

"Challenge Your Challenges" is more than just my platform—it's my story, my voice, and a reflection of who I am. From the moment I was born, I've faced challenge after challenge. But did I let that stop me? No! Through "Challenge Your Challenges," I aim to show people everywhere that you can overcome your obstacles. I want to encourage others to see that each challenge is simply an opportunity to rise above.

> "Your obstacle is just an opportunity for you to overcome"
>
> —Alexis R. Lowry

In 2017, doctors diagnosed me with vocal paralysis. One vocal cord could not move, and the other had little to no movement. They told me I would never be able to sing and were surprised I could speak as well as I could. I am now the reigning North Carolina Senior Beta Club Champion of Solo, Duo, and Trio–Vocalist, and I am one of the 0.2% of Native Americans who sing opera. This is one of many reminders for me that there is nothing my God cannot do. For me, this was a hard challenge—having to go to vocal therapy to strengthen my vocal cords. But all the therapy sessions were so rewarding because I can now see the fruit of my hard work and dedication in making my vocal cords stronger.

In 2019, I faced one of the hardest challenges I've ever encountered: being diagnosed with scoliosis. I wore a hard Boston back brace for twenty-two hours a day. As an 11-year-old girl in 6th grade, this was not how I had planned my middle school years. I was going to "fit in," wear the cutest outfits, and make my junior high school friends. Instead, I was stuck with a back brace. I had to relearn how to pick things up off the floor, I didn't have many friends because they looked at me differently, and I had to wear baggy clothes to accommodate my brace.

Then, if that wasn't enough, in the spring of my 6th grade year, the world was hit by the COVID-19 pandemic. In a way, I am grateful for the isolation the pandemic gave me, as it gave me the opportunity to seek Jesus and lean on Him. During the pandemic, my classes were online, so I could hide the disorder behind my computer screen. I have always loved music and theatrics, so I didn't give that up because of COVID-19. During that time, I was still bullied, and the stares and comments continued. I began to become numb to the negativity, believing the negative words others spoke about me.

I felt crippled by the weight of the negative words, and no matter how hard I tried, I couldn't shake off the hurtful comments from kids and an instructor who didn't even know my story.

Did you catch something? "I couldn't." I did have one thing right: I couldn't shake off the pain. But I know someone who can heal the deepest wounds and shake off the pain—someone who gives joy for mourning and turns our ashes into beauty. That someone is Jesus. I was raised in church and knew who God, Jesus, and the Holy Spirit were. During church services, I heard people share their testimonies of how God brought them through their storms. But it wasn't until I went through this specific storm in my life that I realized just how God brought me from Glory to Glory. It makes me really ponder the thought of why the Angels never stop singing "Holy." Because that is who God is. He is Holy and Worthy to be praised.

But in 2021, when I was at one of the lowest points in my life, I was tired of being tired, to say the least, and I didn't have any more tears left in me. I could see the fruit of my pain, and I saw God using my pain for His almighty purpose. My purpose with this testimony was to show others that your condition does not define you—God does. And just as it says in Isaiah 40:31, *"But those who wait on the Lord Shall renew their strength; They shall mount up with wings like eagles, they shall run and not be weary, they shall walk and not faint"* (NKJV).

When we remain steadfast with hope and perseverance in God, He will give us strength to carry on. Even during my battle with my diagnosis of scoliosis, I never lost hope in God. Was it hard?

Yes. Did I question God on why I was dealing with bullying on top of scoliosis? Absolutely. But did my hope ever waver? No; because, as it says in Isaiah 53:5, *"By His wounds we are healed"* (ESV), and my hope was found in God's perfect love and peace.

In March of 2021, I went to the doctor for my scoliosis check-up. He said my spinal curve had increased from 40 degrees to 65 degrees, and that I would have to have surgery. There was no other form of treatment, other than surgery. I knew there was a high risk of complications concerning the surgery. They had scheduled me for surgery on May 28, 2021 (remember that date), but my family and I would never accept that diagnosis, let alone that I had to have surgery.

We started praying and persevering in the waiting. We were connected to a doctor in Alabama, who was a well-known holistic care doctor. But he could not take my case, and I felt like I hit a brick wall. The doctor mentioned, "I know someone who is one of the greatest in his field dealing with holistic care and scoliosis. He has been working for over 30 years and has never had to send a person to surgery." In amazement, I said, "I see You, God!" So, we flew out to Minneapolis, Minnesota, and I started holistic therapy.

And on May 28, 2021, in St. Cloud, Minnesota, this girl was getting her healing. By the time we left Minnesota, I was no longer on the waitlist for surgery, and my 1-inch difference in leg length was gone. Doctors are still amazed to this day at the miracles and breakthroughs that have happened in my life.

There is so much worth dealing with in the waiting process. Hold fast during the waiting, because your breakthrough is coming. You may feel like you're crumbling and breaking down, but you're breaking through your walls.

Differently Abled

In 2021, God gave me the term "Challenge Your Challenges." In that moment, I knew God was not only telling me this for myself but also to share with the world for such a time as this—a purpose to share that our challenges do not define us—God does. As people, I feel that we tend to carry the weight of the world, and if not the world, we carry the weight of our burdens. I personally know what it's like to carry the weight of my burdens, and it's honestly tiring and painful. Weight is not free; there is a price. But when you come to the realization that God has given you the power to overcome obstacles, freedom and victory are yours.

I personally love the story of Ruth and Naomi, and just to give you a little background: Naomi lived in a country called Moab with her husband Elimelech, their two sons, and their wives. When her husband passed away, they remained in the country for ten years. But after her sons passed away, Naomi decided to return to the land of Judah. Naomi told her two daughters-in-law to leave and return to their mothers' homes. One kissed her and left (Orpah), and the other (Ruth) clung to Naomi. The challenge that stuck out to me was the one Ruth faced. She was a widow in a foreign land, yet she stayed faithful to Naomi. She could have walked away, but she chose to stay. And because she stayed faithful, God rewarded Ruth by placing her in the lineage of David.

I believe we can all take away an important lesson from this story: faithfulness is key when overcoming obstacles. Being faithful in the waiting is crucial. Just as oil is produced from the crushing, so too are we. We must remain in a posture of faithfulness, knowing that there will be ripe fruit borne from our testimony—a plentiful harvest that others will see as the result of hard work and perseverance.

Even in the midst of your obstacle, God will make a way. Just as He did for Ruth, Naomi, Daniel, Esther, Moses, Joseph, and so many more important figures in the Bible.

In 2022, I created my personal platform, "Challenge Your Challenges." I created this platform to inspire others with different abilities to chase after their dreams and to educate others on the importance of supporting those with different abilities. I also aim to encourage individuals that no matter what obstacle or challenge you face, you will overcome it.

When I was diagnosed with scoliosis, one of my biggest challenges was dealing with the word "disabled." If you look up the definition of "disabled," it says, "limits a person." I am a firm believer that there are no limitations in life, and if you set your mind to something, "the sky's the limit."

When I competed in the 2023 Teen Miss Lumbee Pageant, I did it for the little girl inside of me who dreamed of walking on that stage. Ever since I was a little girl, I would look at my Tribal Ambassadors representing with grace and dignity and say, "That will be me." As a young girl, I wanted to compete but couldn't. Why? Because the doctors advised me not to, due to health concerns. Competing in the pageant was one of the hardest but most rewarding things I've ever done. I realized the strength I carried not only as a young Indigenous woman but as a young Indigenous woman overcoming her obstacles.

If we really think about it, we all have a different ability—something we may not be able to do the same as others.

Whether it's a medical condition or an everyday obstacle, like being organized.

My different ability was walking differently due to scoliosis. Because of scoliosis, there is a pinched nerve within my spine that causes my foot not to rotate properly. Through Jesus and vibration therapy, I know and believe that one day it will be corrected. But as of now, I walk differently, and others ask questions and make remarks. But do I let that stop me from achieving my goals? No. Why? Because we will always face obstacles, but it's up to us how we respond to them. I respond with faith, hope, perseverance, and strength found within God. I look at an obstacle not as a wall, but as a door that we can open for the opportunity to grow. Obstacles can be hard, tiring, and painful at times. But one thing I've learned is that your test will turn into a testimony. And your testimony is not wasted; there is a divine purpose within your pain.

Turning your Triggers into a Testimony

On March 10, 2024, I witnessed something that would alter my perspective on life forever. I witnessed a fatal car accident that led to a fatality caused by a drunk driver. As a new driver, I never thought this would happen to me. I was approaching a stoplight that turned green before I came to a complete stop in the distance, I could see an SUV approaching on the opposite side of the road at the intersection. When the light turned green, I was about to proceed through the intersection when I heard a soft voice say, "Alexis, wait." This was the Holy Spirit who guided me to proceed with careful reflection it was then, I saw a car speeding through the intersection at about 90 mph, but at that moment I knew they were running a red light. The car that was opposite of me at that intersection proceeded to the middle of the intersection and then an explosion happened. The car T-boned the SUV in front of me and hit the light pole. I saw sparks and heard an indescribable sound; bodies were thrown from the SUV and glass, and metal flew everywhere. I remember seeing car bumpers and glass lying in the middle of road and smoke fill the air. It happened right in front of our bumper, but we did not get hit. I now know that God had a hand of protection all around us. After I pulled over to a safe place all I could do was cry and thank God for His grace and protection on my life and my mother's. I realized that life is not something to take for granted because you can be here one minute and gone the next.

> Side Note: *Life is a gift. Cherish your family, spend every moment to the fullest, and be yourself. Because God only made one of you.*

After witnessing this accident, I went through a period where I didn't want to drive. Even when I would go through that intersection, it pained me. A week later, my mom made me get behind the wheel. She knew that if I didn't, I would never drive again. It was hard passing cars because I was afraid of getting hit. Fear invaded my thoughts, and I was honestly afraid to drive.

One night, not long after the accident, my mom made me drive the same route as the night of the accident. I am so thankful to my mom for pushing me, because without her encouragement and God's peace, I probably wouldn't be driving today. That night, it was the same scenario, but with no cars. "Alabaster Box" by CeCe Winans was playing, and I sobbed and cried again. This time, I was thanking God for the triggers I've experienced since the accident. They were essential for my testimony and necessary for my growth. Just as the song says, I had a box that I brought before the King. It was full of tears, pain, triggers, and fear. God truly gave me beauty for my ashes. Now, I am driving, and I am no longer afraid. All glory to God; I am so grateful for His new mercies, peace, and perfect love.

> Isaiah 61:3 says, *"To console those who mourn in Zion, to give them beauty for ashes, the oil of joy for mourning, the garment of praise for the spirit of heaviness; that they may be called trees of righteousness, the planting of the Lord, that He may be glorified."* (NKJV)

At the 2024 Gather Your Girls Women's Conference at Mt. Olive PH Church, we did a prophetic exchange of our ashes for beauty. When I placed my ashes on the altar, I could see a beautiful garden flourishing. It amazes me that the God of the universe, the King of Kings, would want my ashes. I am forever grateful for His love, which is deeper than any valley and wider than any ocean. Through my challenges, God has truly given me beauty for ashes, the oil of joy for mourning, and the garment of praise for the spirit of heaviness.

I am truly not a perfect person; I have made mistakes and been through hard obstacles. I have not been defeated by life's challenges, but I am just a girl who has learned to challenge her challenges. Through every mountain I've climbed and valley I've walked through, I have learned that nothing is wasted—not even the tears. Every piece is part of the beautiful story that Yahweh (God) is writing, and it is a story that will encourage others to rise and challenge their challenges.

Daughter of the King

Alexis Rosa Lowry, 16, is a distinguished servant leader and opera vocalist whose faith and academic excellence underpin her success. As the inaugural Miss Indigenous North Carolina Ambassador, her platform, "Challenge Your Challenges," empowers others to overcome adversity. A published author and aspiring orthodontist, Alexis exemplifies leadership, service, and resilience.

16

GRACED TO GRIEVE

Grief Unforeseen

Dr. Deborah C Anthony

The journey through grief is one of life's most challenging and transformative experiences. It strikes unexpectedly, disrupting the very fabric of our existence and leaving us grappling with profound emotions we never anticipated. Imagine the innocence of a child, moving through life untouched by sorrow, only to be confronted later with the harsh reality of loss. This is an invitation to delve into the complexities of grief, to understand its varied forms, and to ultimately learn how to navigate its challenging waters with grace and resilience.

Grief, they say, is an inevitable companion—a family member we cannot shake off, a constant presence in our lives. I invite you to join me as I share my encounters with grief, hoping my stories will serve as beacons of insight for your journey. Whether it's the loss of a job, the dissolution of a marriage, the fracture of a friendship, or the passing of a loved one, grief finds us in myriad ways, carving hollows in our hearts and reshaping our understanding of life's fragility.

The word "grief" can be daunting—an unwelcome disruptor that crashes into our lives at inconvenient times. It demands attention, refusing to be ignored or suppressed. Is there a right way to grieve? Can lessons or tools prepare us for this inevitable human experience? These are the questions that drive us to seek understanding and guidance.

Who truly wakes up prepared to discuss grief? Yet, it's an inescapable companion, a shadow that darkens our doorsteps at the most unexpected moments. The journey through grief is undeniably one of life's most challenging and transformative experiences. It disrupts the very fabric of our existence, stirring profound emotions we never anticipated and often feel unprepared to handle.

My confrontation with grief came abruptly and painfully on November 8, 2021, a date that forever altered the landscape of my life. It was on this night that my son tragically ended his life. The shock was palpable—a visceral, soul-crushing blow that left me grappling with an immense void. I had faced losses before—jobs, relationships, and friendships had come and gone, each departure etching a mark of sorrow upon my heart. Yet, none compared to the seismic shift caused by the loss of my child. This was not just another grief; this was a profound upheaval that forced me to stop and reevaluate everything I knew about mourning, pain, and survival.

This chapter, born from the deepest wells of personal anguish, seeks to invite you into an exploration of grief—not just as a concept but as a profoundly personal experience that varies in shape and intensity for each of us. If you find yourself questioning whether I truly grasp the full impact of the "G-word," let me assure you, I do. My aim is not only to share my journey but to resonate deeply with yours, to validate the reality of your loss, no matter the scale. Your loss is significant because it was significant to you; it is not the size of the loss that defines its impact but the depth of the bond that was severed.

Grief is an inevitable shadow that follows us throughout life—a family member we did not choose, a constant, sometimes unwelcome presence that shapes our existence. In the following pages, we will delve deeply into the multifaceted nature of grief, exploring its emotional, physical, cognitive, and spiritual dimensions. We will learn together how to navigate the tumultuous waters of mourning, find ways to give voice to our pain, acknowledge the reality of our suffering, and gradually reclaim the pieces of our shattered lives.

Defining Grief with Clarity and Compassion:

Grief is the complex response to loss encompassing a wide range of emotional, physical, cognitive, and spiritual reactions. It is the internal meaning attached to the experience of loss. This book challenges the myth that grief must be tied to monumental losses like death or divorce. Even subtle losses can trigger grieving processes, revealing the often-overlooked impact of seemingly minor separations or changes in our lives.

Children, for example, might not remember a parent they lost at an early age. Still, the void left by that absence can manifest in unexplained sadness or emotional gaps that later life events might exacerbate or illuminate. It's essential to dispel the notion that one person's grief is more or less significant than another's. Grief is personal and real, regardless of its' source or scope.

The first wave of grief that struck me when I lost my son was one of disbelief. I did not want to accept that this reality was mine to bear. I found myself oscillating between shock and profound sorrow, struggling to make sense of the irreparable rupture in the fabric of my life. It's crucial to understand that God-crafted emotions are integral to our being. Acknowledging and expressing these emotions is not only healthy but necessary for healing. Yet, it's also important to recognize when emotions spiral out of control, dictating actions that may not serve us well in the long term.

The Catalyst of Personal Loss

In the late autumn of 2021, a shift occurred in my life—a shift that began as an insistent inner voice urging me to return home from a work trip. This intuitive call, which I later recognized as a divine warning, began a deeply personal journey into understanding grief. My son, John Wesley Christian Anthony, only 18 years old, was silently battling a storm of depression and hopelessness that I was yet to comprehend fully.

Reflecting on that weekend, I remember the unsettling feeling that washed over me—a mother's instinct that something was amiss. Despite the physical distance, my heart was tethered to home, to my children, and most poignantly, to John, whose struggles I had only begun to glimpse. The urgency in that divine whisper, "Go home," became the last thread pulling me back to the moments leading up to the tragedy.

The Voice That Guided Me Home

Upon changing my flight and returning on Saturday night, I was enveloped by a superficial calm that belied the underlying turmoil. My arrival was met with normalcy, yet the pit in my stomach grew as intuitive discomfort mingled with confusion. Why was this unease so persistent? What was I missing? These questions haunted me as I tried to anchor myself in the familiarity of family and routine.

The next morning, a directive to spend time with my children overrode my usual Sunday plans. This rare alignment—having all six children together for breakfast—seemed a perfect opportunity for bonding. Yet, John's uncharacteristic quietness and detachment during the meal hinted at deeper issues, which I initially misread as mere fatigue.

The Unseen Battle

As the day unfolded, I was unaware that I was witnessing the final hours of normalcy with my son. John's reluctance to accompany us to drop off his sister at college was a crack in the facade, revealing a glimpse of his internal struggle. The tension in the car, his silent brooding—these were signs I would only fully understand in retrospect.

Our return home that afternoon was shadowed by an ominous vision that struck me—a premonition of death that sent chills down my spine and propelled me into prayer. The fear was palpable, yet its target was unknown. This surreal moment of foreboding left me grappling with a nebulous threat looming over my family.

The Moment That Changed Everything

That evening, the routine was comforting yet deceptive. John's act of fetching dinner for the family was a mask of normalcy that concealed his fatal intentions. His final goodnight, imbued with love and an almost palpable sense of finality, is a memory that I hold with both profound sorrow and deep love. It was a goodbye disguised as an ordinary moment, one that left a permanent imprint on my soul.

Reflection and Realization

In the aftermath of John's death, I found myself dissecting every interaction, every missed sign. The quiet despair that had enveloped him was a battle he fought largely in silence, masked by the veneer of daily life and adolescent routines. The signs—his withdrawal, his silent cries for help, his disconnection from life—were there, yet they were signals I could not fully decode at the time.

The impact of the pandemic—social isolation, disrupted routines, and heightened anxieties—had exacerbated his underlying issues. Like many others, my son found himself lost in the shuffle of life's demands, retreating increasingly into a digital world where I struggled to follow. I hold to this quote by David Kessler:

"Remember with More Love than Pain—When a loved one dies by suicide, it feels like we will never be the same. And in truth, we won't be. The grief will always be there, but we can heal and begin to build a life of love around the loss."

The Need for a Biblical Understanding of Grief

This personal tragedy underscored a critical gap in our approach to grief and mourning. The existing paradigms, both secular and within faith communities, seemed inadequate, lacking a framework that fully embraced the spiritual dimensions of healing. The governance of grief is impossible without the sustaining power of God's grace. Isaiah 53:4 tells us that Jesus *"borne our griefs and carried our sorrows"* (KJV), indicating that through His sacrifice, believers are offered the grace to govern their grief.

- **God's Grace as a Governing Force:** God's grace is central to managing grief. It provides the strength to continue living despite loss, allowing individuals to process their pain without being consumed by it. Grace acts as the foundation for spiritual and emotional governance, offering comfort and the power to heal.

- **The Exchange of Grief for Grace:** The Bible promises an exchange of beauty for ashes and joy for mourning in Isaiah 61:3. This divine exchange is an example of how grace transforms the grieving process. Through grace, sorrow does not have to dictate a person's life, and healing can occur even in the midst of profound loss. Grace provides the structure and support needed to guide the grieving heart toward hope and renewal.

Grief and the Need for Emotional Regulation

Emotional regulation is a key aspect of governing grief. Extreme emotional responses—ranging from sadness and anger to numbness—are common during grief. However, without proper regulation, these emotions can lead to emotional instability and poor decision-making.

Emotional Health and Grief: Managing emotions during grief is essential for maintaining mental and emotional well-being. Individuals may find themselves reacting to grief in unpredictable ways, which can strain relationships and lead to further emotional distress.

Self-Governance in Emotional Overwhelm: Learning to recognize and manage emotions without being overtaken by them is critical. This involves engaging in practices like prayer and meditation and leaning on biblical principles to maintain balance and perspective. Philippians 4:6-7 encourages believers to bring their anxieties to God through prayer, promising peace that transcends understanding—a crucial step in governing emotional responses during grief.

Spiritual Authority in Grief: Reclaiming Dominion

The Bible teaches that God has given believers authority over their emotions and circumstances through Christ. 2 Corinthians 10:5 tells believers to take every thought captive, bringing it under the authority of Christ.

Taking Authority Over Grief: Governing grief means reclaiming spiritual authority over thoughts and emotions. This does not mean suppressing feelings but rather exercising control over how emotions are processed and expressed. Grief should not be allowed to spiral into despair, as God has equipped believers to govern their emotional states.

Jesus' Example of Governing Grief: John 11:35 shows Jesus weeping over Lazarus' death. He grieves but does not remain in a state of despair. Instead, He moves forward and performs a miracle. This example demonstrates the balance of feeling grief without being ruled by it, showing that governing grief does not mean avoiding emotions but directing them in a way that leads to healing.

Governing Grief Through Biblical Discipline

Discipline is an essential part of governing grief. The Bible encourages believers to take control of their thoughts and emotions, renewing their minds through Christ.

Disciplining the Mind and Spirit: Romans 12:2 reminds believers to be transformed by the renewing of their minds. During grief, negative or despairing thoughts can easily take hold. Governing grief involves actively engaging in practices that prevent these thoughts from becoming dominant.

Tools for Governing Grief:

- **Prayer and Devotion:** Regular prayer and devotion provide a framework for processing grief in a healthy way.
- **Community Support:** Leaning on spiritual leaders and trusted friends can help individuals remain grounded in faith, offering accountability and support.
- **Scripture:** The use of biblical promises and truths, such as Psalm 23, guides individuals through the grieving process with the assurance of God's presence and comfort.

The Purpose of Governing Grief: Healing and Transformation

When grief is governed, it becomes a tool for healing rather than a source of prolonged pain.

Healing Through Governance: Properly governed grief allows space for reflection, learning, and eventual restoration. It helps individuals process their sorrow constructively, leading to emotional and spiritual healing.

Transformation Through Governed Grief: God uses grief as part of His refining process, and when governed with grace, grief can lead to personal and spiritual transformation. Individuals often emerge from grief with a deeper relationship with God and a renewed sense of purpose.

Grief, when governed by God's grace, becomes a journey toward healing and transformation. The necessity of governing grief is evident in how the government protects emotional, spiritual, and mental health. As believers, we are called to exercise spiritual authority over our emotions, allowing God's grace to lead us through the valley of sorrow and into a place of restoration. Grieving with grace, rather than being consumed by sorrow, opens the door to deeper healing, spiritual growth, and a more profound experience of God's presence.

By reframing grief as an opportunity to experience God's grace, the Christian community is equipped to offer support and guidance to those navigating the difficult journey of loss. Grief does not need to control our lives; with God's grace, we can govern it and find healing, hope, and transformation.

Dr Deborah C Anthony has dedicated her life to serving the Lord with joy. She shares over 24 years of marriage with her husband, John Anthony, and cherishes their six children, including a son now with the Lord, and her grandson. Combining corporate success with Kingdom purpose, Deborah leads iEmerge Academy, a leadership development program advancing leaders and organizations. As the author of six devotionals and leadership books, her faith-driven words inspire countless lives. Through her unwavering dedication to faith, family, and leadership, Deborah's journey continues to empower generations.

Discover more at
www.deborahcanthony.com.

GLOBAL PERSPECTIVE TO GOVERN

17
GRACED FOR COUNSEL

Entering the Secret Counsel of the Lord

Apostle Sharlina Mack

Many years ago, I embarked on this journey, seeking clarity and understanding about the Lord God Almighty. Along the way, it was revealed to me that there are various realms of counsel and guidance available to us:

1. The **Safety in the Multitude of Counsel**
2. The **Secret Counsel of the Lord**
3. The **Secret Counsel of Satan**
4. The **School of the Holy Spirit**

The mandate to teach my children and the generations that follow about these realms has been burning in my heart for over 15 years. I have worked with community leaders to help parents, children, and families attain and reach the Secret Counsel of the Lord, emphasizing that there must be a level of spiritual maturity beyond mere discipleship.

To access the Secret Counsel of the Lord, one must attain a status of sonship or friendship with God. As Jesus said in John 15:15, *"No longer do I call you servants... but I have called you friends"* (NKJV). These sessions with the Lord occur whenever He calls them, and we must be willing to surrender to the leading of the Holy Spirit to grow and mature appropriately.

There are stages of spiritual growth and maturity where the consecrated but imperfect person surrenders to the will of the Lord for their lives. One such stage is enrollment in the **School of the Holy Spirit**. I have spent over ten years being trained and spiritually developed by the Holy Spirit to serve, lead, and be God's friend.

In the School of the Holy Spirit, individuals are trained by the Lord to fill the necessary gaps due to trauma and neglect. The Holy Spirit dwells in those broken and wounded areas of our lives, teaching, training, and equipping us with the tools and equipment needed to fulfill our purpose. Often, tribulations and trials arise from unresolved trauma, requiring us to invite the Holy Spirit into those spaces for healing.

Entering the Secret Counsel of the Lord

In the Secret Counsel of the Lord, meetings or sessions can be called upon us by the Lord at any time and place on earth. When these sessions are called, we must be willing to surrender to the leading of the Holy Spirit. This place requires total surrender of our will, mission, and vision for the will of God in our lives.

Great things occur in the Secret Counsel of the Lord. In this sacred space:

- We can bring any questions, issues, or offenses we need to address.
- The Lord provokes us to commune with Him to resolve these matters.
- Revelations are given to connect previous trials, offering wisdom to assist us in completing our assignments.
- It's a place of continual spiritual growth and development.
- Visions, missions, purposes, plans, and strategies are developed.
- Divine downloads, such as books and remedies, are received.
- We find rest, peace of mind, and what some call the "fountain of youth," as God renews us and grants us access to greater levels of intellectual clarity and revelation.

Conversations with the Lord in this place provide guidance and instructions for healing and deliverance, preparing us to overcome present trials and embrace the future.

The School of the Holy Spirit

The School of the Holy Spirit trains, prepares, and equips us to enter the Secret Counsel of the Lord. Physical age does not limit entry; rather, the person must comprehend and understand the will of God and be able to surrender their will for the perfect—not just the permissive—will of God.

Understanding Shame and Healing from Trauma

Shame, guilt, and embarrassment are normal human emotions that, in themselves, are not evil. However, they can be misinterpreted when we don't understand their foundational purposes. I learned that shame is designed to teach and correct beliefs and change behaviors.

Many feel shame because they carry the weight of offenses committed against them, not realizing that the shame truly belongs to the offender. When I had this revelation, I understood that I was still feeling shame about past traumas that were not my fault. Recognizing this allowed me to begin the healing process.

God created both good and evil (Isaiah 45:7) and understanding this helps us comprehend the nature of our struggles. The adversary operates within the realm of evil, but he requires permission to tempt and try us. Our victory comes through Jesus Christ and His redeeming blood (Revelation 12:11).

The Battle Between Sin and Righteousness

Sin is not merely the opposite of salvation; it has its own set of rules and laws. It's a form of government and kingdom citizenship that does not welcome illegal immigrants. As citizens of the Kingdom of God, we are not designed to live in sin. When we trespass into sin, we experience torment and anguish because we are dwelling where we do not belong.

The adversary, Satan, knows the rules and is the ruler over the domain of sin. His goal is to make us, as Kingdom citizens, uncomfortable until we submit to becoming citizens of his realm. He keeps the pathways to sin entertaining and captivating, hoping we lose focus and cross over into his territory.

Redemption Through Christ

Jesus Christ is our Redeemer and the way back to righteousness. His redemption from sin and its torment cannot be activated until we accept Him as Lord and Savior. When we accept Christ, we gain Kingdom citizenship with benefits that daily load us (Psalm 68:19). However, we must receive and activate these benefits by embracing the Holy Spirit and allowing Him to work in our lives.

As believers, we must understand that when we trespass into sin, Christ cannot cross those borders to retrieve us unless we repent and return to Him. It's similar to how a country cannot negotiate for the safe return of someone who is not its' citizen. We must maintain our citizenship in the Kingdom of God.

The Trials of Our Faith

Trials are designed to teach, train, and equip us, revealing beliefs that provoke behaviors leading to our struggles. James 1:2-4 reminds us that the testing of our faith produces patience, leading us to maturity. Instead of seeking quick fixes, we should desire what God has planned for us, understanding that trials come to make us stronger.

When we recognize we're in a trial, it's essential to ask the Lord:

- **Who** is allowing this process?
- **What** have I or my ancestors done that granted access to this trial?
- **When** will the trial be over?
- **Where** should I place my petitions—on the altar of the Lord or elsewhere?
- **Why** am I entering this trial?
- **How** does this trial connect to the vision and plan God has for me?

By seeking God's perspective, we gain wisdom and understanding, allowing us to grow and mature spiritually.

Embracing Our Kingdom Citizenship

God has mandated me to learn and teach others how to use their gifts as they receive the Holy Spirit, helping them find and fulfill their destinies and purposes. We must be aware that the enemy will always have boundary patrols. When we cross into sin, we risk trauma and abuse because we're in territory where we do not belong.

However, through Christ, we have the power to resist sin and reverse generational curses. The redemption offered by Jesus allows us to overcome the government of sin and live in the freedom of righteousness.

Our journey involves continual growth, surrender, and reliance on the Lord. By entering the Secret Counsel of the Lord and embracing the training of the Holy Spirit, we position ourselves to receive divine guidance, healing, and revelation. We learn to navigate trials with wisdom, understanding that they serve a greater purpose in God's plan for our lives.

May we all seek to mature spiritually, surrender our wills for God's perfect will, and walk confidently in our Kingdom citizenship. Let us embrace the grace to govern our lives according to His purpose, experiencing the fullness of His love, peace, and joy.

Apostle Sharlina Pye Mack, J.D. is a licensed and ordained minister, attorney, mediator, coach and teacher. She has coached youth and been actively involved in ministry for over 30 years. She is mandated to teach others how to Grow to Walk together and begin to Work to Gather.

18

GRACED TO DISTRIBUTE

Willing to Grant Grace

Apostle Dr. Kimberly L. McClinton

Grace is not pretty to the one bestowing it. Grace often comes with the shedding of blood, sacrifice, humility, and saving face. It can cause the giver to experience extreme heights and depths of pain. Grace will cause a person to go beyond themselves to give. For the one receiving grace, it ends anxiety and fear and issues a prize, often undeservingly. The receiver must no longer endure a dreaded outcome, punishment, or consequences because grace was extended.

The distributor of grace must remember that all grace comes through that same pathway. Some went to extremes to issue grace;

through time and growth, they were entrusted with the ability to issue grace. To be willing to issue grace, the bestower recognizes that they received this gift and must be willing to share it with someone else. I remember a message in which the preacher said grace is getting what you do not deserve, and mercy is not getting what you deserve.

My Story

At the beginning of my ministry, I never saw myself in the position of covering for others. I always figured I would help others and remain in the background, figuring things out. From this vantage point, I didn't see what it takes to govern; I saw only how to create a space and produce the desired outcome. While I was helping, I saw grace extended to those who did not deserve it. I was more focused on the assignments and glorifying the image of man more than God. I did not consider the ultimate needs of the people.

After years in ministry, I have learned that if our objective is not glorifying God and pointing people back to the Father, our provider, we govern within another kingdom. My initial perspective came from a willingness to serve. However, I became frustrated with people's desire to receive and not give anything in return.

Moses missed God because he responded to the people and became frustrated instead of issuing grace (Numbers 20:10-13). I won't ever forget my growing pains in issuing grace. There was a sister I looked up to, but she was exposed in a moment of sin. Her exposure was public, causing pain and dishonor. I looked down at her and asked, "How could you?"

However, a year later, I ended up in the same predicament, in different circumstances, yet with the same sin. I had to ask myself how I could get into this position. How did I allow this and fail to exercise self-control? Then I learned the true meaning of Galatians 6:1-3, *"Brethren, if a man is overtaken in any trespass, you who are spiritual restore such a one in a spirit of gentleness, considering yourself lest you also be tempted"* (NKJV).

I began to understand that I needed grace extended to me to be restored. I was thankful I received it and had an opportunity to ask that sister for forgiveness for how I treated her because I had not willingly extended grace.

Support

Scripture teaches grace consistently. In Mark 6, we see an example of a miracle of provision to a massive number of people. The people were with Jesus for three days, fasting as he ministered to them. Finally, he told his disciples not to send them away without feeding them. This was an example of a leader extending grace. The disciples were opposed and said: *"This is a deserted place, and already the hour is late. Send them away, that they may go into the surrounding country and villages and buy themselves bread; for they have nothing to eat. But He answered and said to them, You give them something to eat"* (Mark 6:35-38, NKJV).

Often, we hold events but don't want to feed the people's bodily needs. We complain and resent the cost of feeding the masses. We are not giving Jesus the opportunity to work a miracle through us. He was attempting to demonstrate grace, love, and care and allow the disciples to participate with him.

We often ignore small yet great miracles by staying focused on our frustration instead of rejoicing that God desires to work with and through us. Although the miracle occurred, it seemed insignificant to the disciples since they were more focused on what would happen next. I call it majoring in the minors, missing a moment to govern grace.

Mark records that the leftovers were abundant after the disciples fed them. Then Jesus told his disciples to sail to the other side of the lake. While in the boat, Jesus prays as they experience turbulence. They only see the exterior reality; they never see Jesus working through them, which causes them to miss what God is trying to have them (and us) understand.

There is grace for all who need grace. He will use your hand. He will use you to perform and provide. Do not overlook what God does through your hand; don't glory in it. Stay humble before our King. Missed moments with Him are crucial and could devastate our walk with Him. What would have happened had the disciples always been available for grace to work through them?

As leaders who may serve a family or a group, we must understand and always remember that God is not miserly with His promises. He desires us to demonstrate Himself through you so that others learn and come to know Him. His words are more than just a great story. He expects us to do the same work because we partner with Him willingly. We are vessels for Him to use to reach greater levels and masses of people.

In this example in Mark 6, we see it's desirable to hold a three-day revival or meeting where people are taught and trained and prayerfully understand the King and His everlasting kingdom.

It is evident when the Lord tries to drive something home with us. For example, he says, as he did in Revelation 2:7 and Matthew 11:15, *"He that hath an ear, let him hear"* (KJV). He tells us there is more to this scenario than just what you see. There's activity going on, and if you are sensitive in the spirit, you will hear beyond words. You will receive the instruction and insight necessary to fulfill His will and His way. We may overlook miracles upon miracles because we're focused on those who we genuinely want to see. But if we begin to open our eyes to recognize God's presence, influence, and inner workings in our lives, we will be more humble and ready for him at any moment.

You, too, can feed 4,000 people with a small amount that becomes greater because you put it in the hands of the Lord with thankfulness. This is no small feat. As humans, we can sometimes take for granted the things of the Lord. Minor steps, such as extending grace to satisfy the body's needs, were necessary to complete the Lord's demonstration.

We will see hearts and minds change when we comprehend that God wants to extend His grace to the world through His people. The disciples were amazed when Jesus commanded the wind and the sea, but they missed His miracle of feeding thousands of people with few provisions. When we submit to God, our natural needs can be satisfied.

Often, we rationalize the need to extend grace. We think it must make sense to us to extend it. However, God's process of extending grace does not make sense to man's standards. God's way is much higher than our way. His thoughts are much higher than our thoughts.

At times, we feel that people do not deserve the benefit of the doubt or the grace that we can bestow on them. However, when we deny access to grace, we are denying love. 1 Corinthians 13:6 shares with us what love is and is not: "*. . . but have not love, it profits me nothing*" (KJV).

We must observe Christ's expectation of us as we have freely received; we need to freely give even if this gift is undeserved. Whether it's deserved or undeserved is not our decision to make. Whoa! I know that was loaded; I felt it, too. Just freely distribute and keep teaching and loving. The responsibility of worth or waste is up to God. He will resolve and settle accounts in His own time. This is one of the most challenging areas for us. Just focus on always being open to issue grace and let God take care of His part.

I am reminded of the parable in Matthew 18:21-35; a servant must answer to his master and beg for mercy as he does not have the funds to settle his debt. The master releases him from it. This newly freed man who received grace then goes to the person owing him, and instead of reciprocating what he just received, he is harsh and brutal towards the person. His master then accuses him and punishes him harshly.

So, I encourage the next generation of leaders to be mindful of what Paul said in Galatians 6:1-2, "*Brethren, if a man is overtaken in any trespass, you who are spiritual restore such a one in a spirit of gentleness, considering yourself lest you also be tempted*" (NKJV).

This example of grace keeps me humble to partner with God and my brothers and sisters. Your bestowing grace could save a person's life. Determine to be the example of, in Paul's words, one who reads, hears and governs grace well.

Apostle Kimberly L. McClinton, PhD, is a devoted servant of Christ with over 30 years of ministry experience. She serves globally as an Apostle, preacher, and teacher. She is a wife of 38 years, mother of 3 and grandmother of 12. Apostle McClinton is also a published author, entrepreneur, and educator, committed to advancing God's work of reconciliation.

19

GRACED TO UNIFY

Governing through Grace

Prophet Tracy Manning

We govern through grace, for this is our posture in the kingdom of God. This kingdom of God is often described as God the Ruler.

I believe as Christians we are the ecclesia, the remnant, the chosen. All were called, but few were chosen; this book was intended with you in mind. I wrote this chapter to be effective in the Kingdom of God; we need to uproot all forms of division. Our standards as Christians should be love without boundaries. We must govern through grace. Matthew 6:33 (NKJV) says,

"Seek ye first the Kingdom of God and his righteousness and all these things shall be added to you."

This implies God empowers you to overcome all obstacles and hindrances, including division, prejudice, and racism.

This will be obtainable only through grace. In compliance, you can live in peace and unity. John 14:27 (NKJV), *"Peace I leave with you, my peace I give to you; not as the world gives do I give to you. Let not your heart be troubled, neither let it be afraid."* As I meditated on God's Word, I realized the kingdom suffers violently. This has caused fear and division to sneak into the body of Christ. It's like an underlying illness, which we as the body of Christ, need to address.

Matthew 13:25-30 (NKJV), *"But while men slept, his enemy came and sowed tares among the wheat and went his way. But when the grain had sprouted and produced a crop, then the tares also appeared. So, the servants of the owner came and said to him, 'Sir, did you not sow good seed in your field? How then does it have tares?' He said to them, 'An enemy has done this'. The servants said to him, 'Do you want us then to go and gather them up?' But he said, 'No, lest while you gather up the tares you also uproot the wheat with them. Let both grow together until the harvest, and at the time of harvest I will say to the reapers, 'First gather together the tares and bind them in bundles to burn them but gather the wheat into my barn.'"*

What if the bundles of wheat and tares were in the form of love and hate or division and unity? Grace is the ability to learn and apply that which you didn't know. It requires you to be willing to live and teach others how to take off the old nature and put on the new learned nature. This would edify the Kingdom of God. Grace is not a ticket to sin. It is a ticket to win. When I became a believer, I didn't realize all my obstacles didn't die. I still had an underlying illness, although I knew that Jesus would heal it. Eventually, I realized I would never achieve the outcome I wanted if I did not learn how to trust Him through grace. I overcame difficult obstacles by understanding not my will, but His will be done. God's grace is sufficient. We need to think soberly, not drunkenly. According to Philippians 1:6 (NKJV), *"Being confident of this very thing, that He who has begun a good work in you will complete it until the day of Jesus Christ."* It's time to stand up and allow God to get rid of the tares that will separate us from the love of God. Matthew 11:12 (NKJV), *"…and from the days of John the Baptist until now the kingdom of heaven suffers violence, and the violent take it by force."* Because we Christians won't talk about this, we have, in fact, enforced division and hate. I was one of these many believers in pain and distrust and with no peace even though I was in the body of Christ.

You may think, just as I did, this division will last forever. You may be right. If I rewrite this book from a worldly perspective, a life without God, then I think of Proverbs 14:12 (NKJV), *"There is a way that seems right to a man, but its end is the way of death."* I can testify about a house divided by racism. My husband and I, as pastor, had our ministry in North Aurora, IL. After three years our small church had grown out of space.

I went to work at a soap company where several employees were prejudiced. This was a hostile work environment for African Americans. At one point a white supremacist signed on my desk. I wrote complaints to my union steward, but nothing was resolved. The situation grew even worse. One morning, I left work, and my car's tire had been flattened; I believe this was a threat to keep my mouth shut. As fear grew in me, I heard the Lord say, "I did not give you a spirit of fear but of power, love and a sound mind." My faith grew. After almost one month of fighting with worldly practices, I could see people didn't want to get involved even though they knew this other group was prejudiced. They feared losing their jobs.

I quieted my spirit, as I remembered Matthew 10:28 (NKJV), *"And do not fear those who kill the body but cannot kill the soul. But rather fear Him who is able to destroy both soul and body in hell."* That's when my husband and I and some members of my church earnestly prayed. I cried out for the peace of God since I had had so many sleepless nights. The word peace is like a sword resonating in my spirit.

On June 23, 2016. I heard a small, still voice echo Psalm 23:4 (NKJV), *"Yea, though I walk through the valley of the shadow of death, I will fear no evil; for You are with me; Your rod and Your staff, they comfort me."* The peace I so badly needed was like a sword, meaning this would not be a quiet situation. As a Christian I was taught always to think that we need to "keep the peace", meaning don't say or do anything but pray. I remembered what Jesus said through a Sunday morning message, Matthew 10:34 (NKJV), *"Do not think that I came to bring peace on earth. I did not come to bring peace but a sword."*

This peace that the Holy Spirit was speaking of would require change. I would have to die to my worldly practices which would have caused me to be quiet and do the required obligations. To win the settlement, I would have sued the business and been willing to deal with all the bureaucracy surrounding compensation. I'm not saying that way is not right, I'm saying this is how God allowed me to learn through God's grace. I needed to see it differently.

God was using this situation in my job to develop His grace. The word grace had a different meaning at this point in my life. I could have chosen to treat them as they treated me, that is, to get even. But I knew this would not produce godly fruit. I could have been short-tempered, full of hate, aggressive and even violent. I would have been quick to speak; I might even have lied and found fault. This would have been a familiar state for me. I could have looked for a lawyer and lost sleep and peace.

I could see myself getting frustrated by going back and forth to court. I kept reliving the moments of this injustice. But He said, "I have something greater for you, this peace I give is not as the world gives." And in Philippians 4:7 (NKJV), *"and the peace of God, which surpasses all understanding, will guard your hearts and minds through Christ Jesus."* I thought if I could maintain the peace of God in my heart, I could fulfill His word. I was able to as I studied in Romans 15:13 (NKJV), *"Now may the God of hope fill you with all joy and peace in believing, that you may abound in hope by the power of the Holy Spirit."* This is when I fully understood how to walk through grace. I knew I could not fight the system of this world with common tools.

You must find a scripture to apply daily that enables you to stay on the course of your deliverance. After I meditated on God's word day and night, finally the day came when the union stewards and some soap company management accompanied me and led me to a room. There, they stated the facts that I had been complaining about earlier in June 2016. They read off statements that I said under pressure, things that I didn't remember saying.

I will never forget the silence in the room when it was my turn to speak; it was like God spoke Himself. I felt a weight leave me as all my fears and anxiety went away. I boldly said, "We all need peace. This is all I want, to work in a safe environment. We say we are an equal employment opportunity, where it's not based on origin, ethnicity, race, or any other thing that brings division. I want us to work in peace. That's it, so that this company can grow to its proper potential."

All the union stewards were amazed at how I managed the situation; this is when I learned it's only through God's grace that we can govern. Where race, religion, origin, or education are not factors, and when we as a people can get along for the sake of the one common denominator, then we can witness the power of God on the earth.

At this time, I had an epiphany, wow! Finally, the kingdom of God could do what it was meant to do which is to allow His love to cast out all fear. Psalm 23:6 (NKJV) says, *"Surely goodness and mercy shall follow me All the days of my life; And I will [dwell in the house of the Lord Forever."* What could happen if I allowed grace to govern through me? I believe grace is a key that unlocks doors. Consider that in John 14:2, *"In My Father's house are many mansions; if it were not so, I would have told you. I go to prepare a place for you.* See Jesus went to prepare a mansion for us. This means this place will have lots of doors to enter, which I believe are opened with grace as the key.

When grace has found its way to your heart, you must be willing to walk through to get the outcome that can unlock the doors of division.

After I passed this test, I realized that our predominantly African American church had outgrown our space. So, my husband and I looked for a new building. God always has a bigger plan when we pass the test.

We ended up in Aurora, IL about ten minutes from where our church of 2500 sq. ft. in North Aurora was located. There was a church of 30,000 sq. feet, mostly white people, who were looking to rent space to another congregation.

My church, Rock For All Ages, rented and occupied space in Living Stone Christian Church in the year of 2020. However, God had an even bigger plan for both our congregations. We obeyed His voice, in our surrendering. We merged, and we became a single entity in our ministries, leaving the former things, including the separation in our churches as Rock for All Ages and Living Stone.

We worked together by depending on our total trust in God and our support of each other with much prayer, fasting and seeking the Lord for direction. I heard the Lord speak this Word (Isaiah 43:18-28, NKJV): *"Do not remember the former things, Nor consider the things of old. Behold, I will do a new thing, now it shall spring forth; Shall you not know it? I will even make a road in the wilderness and rivers in the desert."*

In 2022, together we purchased a 10,000 sq. ft. Building on five acres in Montgomery, Illinois. The new name of our church is Rock Solid Christian Fellowship. We are a multicultural team of pastors and members doing the work of the kingdom, as we allow God the Father, Jesus the Son, and the Holy Spirit to be our example. We co-labor in the ministry, governing through grace in the body of Christ. We work together to raise up mature believers. We live and practice Psalm 127:1 (NKJV): *"Unless the*

Lord build the house, they labor in vain who build it; unless the Lord guards the city, the watchman stays awake in vain."

Rock Solid is not just the name of a building, it's a kingdom culture of people where we deal with everyday challenges. We are training people who are willing to impact a nation, one house at a time. We, the body of Christ, can operate in a multicultural lifestyle, where race, ethnicity, education, or one's opinions, beliefs, origin, doctrine, or politics can permeate the kingdom culture. Kingdom culture people is not a place; we are a people who have been deemed the remnant who God has called and chosen, for such a time as this. However, each situation is different. It might not turn out the way you want, especially when you face division. But remember, as a child of God, you are qualified to unlock doors for people who would never be able to get free on their own.

Even though there will be challenges for obedience is never easy, yet it is so rewarding. Consider what I went through at soap company: I had to endure, like a good solder. It was grace that taught me how to come together in love, unity and peace. This grace is what I leave with you; my hope is that this grace is enough, that you may be willing to die to what you know and live through God's perspective, that much more grace will abound in you. Your thoughts are welcome as you journey through God's grace to govern!

Prophetess Tracy Manning is passionate about praying, prophesying, seeing God's people delivered, and fulfilling God's divine purpose on earth. In 2008 Tracy accepted the call of an evangelist and was ordained as a pastor in 2014 and a Prophet in 2022. Tracy has been actively involved in ministry with her husband, Pastor Shaun, since 2014 and, married 23 years, together for over 30 years. Two adult children and two beautiful granddaughters. Tracy is the founder of Rock of Creative Academy and the overseer of Women of Worth ministries, where she hosts an annual conference that has been a mighty outpouring of the spirit of God. Tracy is the author of *Don't Pat Me To Hell*.

FUTURE HOPE
AND ETERNAL
PERSPECTIVE

20

GRACED TO BELIEVE

Grace for Faith to Still Believe in Miracles

Pastor Kim Robinson

"The validity of the Christian faith rests on one supreme Miracle: the cornerstone upon which the whole superstructure of Christianity rises or falls, depends on the truth of this Miracle - the resurrection of Jesus Christ."

—Kathryn Kuhlman

Reflecting, I am amazed at how deeply my life has been impacted by those who not only believed in but were also witnesses to God's miracle-working power. They were examples to me of what it meant to live in expectation, always believing that nothing is impossible with God. They taught me the importance of living a consecrated life, and a life deeply rooted in faith and obedience to God, to see the miraculous. Because of this, I feel a deep sense of responsibility to keep God's power active in the Church. I hope that by imparting to generations the knowledge and revelation I have seen and experienced, the call to accept His grace to govern His miracle-working power will be accepted.

Faith and Miracles in the Past

Growing up as a child, I was influenced by previous generations who believed in the power of prayer and fasting. Generations who didn't think twice if they were called to a prayer meeting, sometimes an all-night "shut-in" prayer meeting, or asked to join in a fast because they knew the power that was in prayer and fasting. Generations who took their children with them. There were no excuses. Generations who operated in miracles, signs, and wonders. Generations who believed that God not only could, but would, do anything if we would just believe. Generations who believed with God there were no limitations, who believed it was simple…allow God to be God. They were men and women used profoundly and powerfully by God. To the one who received the miracle, it did not seem to matter at all who God used to bring the miracle. They were just happy to receive a miracle.

I still believe in miracles today because of those who showed me what God would do with a willing vessel. These type of men and women who had faith in Jesus Christ is what is missing and what is needed today. These were the real influencers. They had no access to social media but had all access to a Great God.

Personal Encounters with Miracles

My first memory of my eye-witnessing a miracle is when I was around the age of six or seven. My mother took me to an old, tiny church located on a dirt road which was, as we used to say, in the "middle of nowhere." We had only recently started attending church as she had just fully committed to accepting Jesus as her savior earlier that year. I can still remember the smell of the worn wood pews and the scratched, old pine hardwood floors. I remember there were very few in attendance that night, maybe 10. At some point during the service, one of the women there began to yell that her baby was not breathing. The sound of desperation in her voice was so chilling. It very quickly turned to her calling on God to help her as she began to scream her baby was dead. As a very young little girl, I remember being so scared. It seemed as if time stopped, and everyone froze at that moment.

The silence was broken by someone yelling to call 911. You could then hear feet running towards the church office phone. My mother, who was not yet a pastor or even a minister at that time, stood up and told everyone that 911 could be called, but there was no time. She told everyone that they needed to pray now. My mother walked over to the woman holding her unconscious baby and began to command life to come back into the child. It was as if she was not looking at what we all saw, a dead baby. She appeared not to be moved by how long it had been since the baby stopped breathing or the screaming sounds of the mother. She just kept praying and commanding life. I felt it was as if she refused to accept the death of this baby. I remember looking at my mother's face and thinking, "Who is this woman?" I had never seen my mother like this before.

She spoke with what I know now to be such authority. Suddenly, you could hear the sound of the baby gasping for air. You could see the rise and fall of her tiny chest. The baby had come back to life.

Everyone began to praise God. It was as if you could feel something had changed in the atmosphere. I understand now that it was the presence of God who entered that small church that night and resurrected the baby.

The memory has never left me. This experience taught me what God will do with a willing vessel that has the courage to step forward in faith and prayer. It taught me that to see a miracle when we pray, our focus cannot be on the condition but rather on Jesus, the Great Physician. It taught me that when a believer walks in their God given authority, there is a power in their prayer that is released to perform the miraculous.

As I am writing now, God has just given me a revelation. I realize it was not a coincidence, everything with God is always intentional, that the same woman, my mother, who prayed for life back into this baby is the same woman whose baby died four years earlier. That baby was ME! My parents told me that I died, flatlined, in a Baltimore, MD, hospital at age two from bronchial pneumonia. My mother repeatedly told me, throughout my life, about my lengthy stay in the hospital after being resuscitated back to life by the medical staff. It was as if she never wanted me to forget. I have never connected these two miracles until this exact moment.

I believe because my mother saw God perform a miracle for her own daughter, it gave her the faith to believe for that baby that night. Her faith aligned with authority, and she stepped forward believing God to do it again. And, when she witnessed God doing it again, she went from faith to faith (Romans 1:17), a way of living in faith that created or generated more faith. This is what gave her a hunger to see Him do it again and again. Looking back, I believe this is why she kept miracles before her eyes and her children's eyes...my eyes.

As a child, I remember it was an everyday occurrence to see miracles in evangelism services playing on our living room TV. My mother would have my sister, and I constantly sit and watch with her as healings took place in these services. I believe whatever you keep before your eyes is what develops a belief system within you. It is because my mother kept a vision of miracles before her eyes, and our eyes, that we have seen, and experienced God work miracles and why we continue to see miracles today.

Miracles like watching right before our eyes as my grandmother's leg, which was shorter than the other, extended to the length of her longer leg while she lay on the church carpet under the anointing of the Holy Spirit. She had to walk out of the service with her orthotic shoes, one heel much higher than the other, in her hands that night. Miracles like blinded eyes opened during one of our church services about a year ago. No one touched this woman who was visiting our church. She simply sat under the anointing of the service and received her sight back. Miracles like the deaf ears of a young girl opening when she simply touched the clothing of the one ministering that day. Miracles like my own healing journey from twelve years of sickness.

I had visited many doctors all around the state. It seemed hopeless as I remained undiagnosed for the first five years. Insurance had stopped paying, and still no answers for the excruciating pain I endured daily. However, I never stopped believing. I could not afford to. My faith was all I had to see me through. I had seen too many others receive miracles. I had to believe He had ALREADY healed me. I just needed to wait on the manifestation of His healing in my body. I realized that it was a done deal accomplished on the cross. Isaiah 53:5 says, *"But He was wounded for our transgressions, he was bruised for our iniquities; the chastisement of our peace was upon him, And by His stripes, WE ARE HEALED"* (NIV).

I quoted this verse, and others, over and over, every day, whether I felt like it or not. I knew the Word cannot lie. I knew the Word was alive, and when spoken, it had to go to work to perform what it said. I slept with the bible and a red t-shirt that my mother bought me with healing scriptures on it. I wore it almost every night. Was it hard? It was beyond hard. I was in agonizing full body pain every day for years. My mind was under extreme attack. Were there days I wanted to give up? Absolutely, many days. There were even countless times I said to God "I can't do this anymore." But grace would not let me give up or give in. God's grace gave me the ability to do with him what I otherwise could not do without him. I could never have made it twelve years without him. And, because I kept the faith and persevered, I received my healing.

Immediate miracles are wonderful. We are a culture that loves things to happen instantly. But not every miracle happens immediately or instantly. Sometimes, it takes perseverance in our faith, standing on the Word of God, and long-term prayer before we see a miracle. There is something to be said about perseverance. The Bible is clear that it is suffering that produces perseverance

(Romans 5:3). No one likes suffering, but the ability to persevere cannot be produced without it. See, in some things, we just have to outlast the enemy. We know the outcome. We always win. So, it is not the outcome we are fighting for. It is faith we are fighting for. We are to fight the good fight of faith.

Obstacles to Miracles Today

With all I have seen and experienced of God's miracle-working power, the question becomes, why are miracles not as prevalent in the church as they have been in the past? I believe that one missing key is a lack of faith in the Church. The bible says that Jesus could not even do many miracles in his own hometown of Nazareth because of their unbelief (Matthew 13:58). He was Jesus, God in the flesh, and their unbelief hindered him from doing miracles. If unbelief hindered Jesus, unbelief certainly is a hindrance today. Belief is necessary to see miracles.

My mother had a saying that I will never forget. She would hold her bible up and say, "I believe every word from Genesis to the globes" (Bibles back then used to have maps in the back of the bible). She was making a declaration that if it was in the bible, then she believed it from the beginning to the end. Jesus is the same yesterday, today and forever. He has not stopped performing miracles. We must believe that if he did it then, he would still do it today.

Another reason I feel we are not seeing miracles today, like before, is because the church as a whole is not walking in our position of authority. To walk in spiritual authority, we must first be submissive to God's authority through obedience. There is a divine order to authority. Authority flows downward. God is the head of Christ; Christ is the head of the church. In the church, God gave overseers or pastors to be shepherds of the church of God. This is the order. Jesus said in John 5:30 he could do nothing on his own because he did not seek his own will but the will of him who sent him. Just as Jesus submitted to God, we must be submissive to God's order of authority to receive God's power. Authority and power go hand in hand.

The story of the centurion in Matthew chapter 8:5-13 is an example of authority and power. The centurion seeks Jesus out because his servant is sick. He tells Jesus he is a man under authority with soldiers under him, and if he says, "Go," they go, "Come," they come, "Do this," they do it. The centurion was exhibiting his faith by his recognition that Jesus was also a man under authority with power who, he believed, could tell the spirit of infirmity to go from his servant, and it would have to go. In response, Jesus said to those following him that he has not found anyone in Israel with such great faith. Our submission to authority is proof of our faith in God. When we all, as believers individually submit to authority, it brings back order to the Church which, in turn, creates a shared faith.

Another obstacle to seeing miracles, I believe, has been the Church's resistance to shift from believing "God can" to believing "God will." There is a big difference between "can" and "will." To say God can is to say it is possible. To say God will moves us from possibility to certainty. It challenges us to step out of our comfort zone. We have become all too comfortable with just believing He can. To say, "He will," not only demands us to step out of our comfort zone, but it also requires us to confront the level of disbelief we find in modern Christianity. To see the miraculous, it is essential that believers make a conscious decision and resolve to remove all doubt, choosing to believe, no matter what it looks like, God will do it.

When I was pregnant with my youngest child, a 3-D scan revealed a cyst on her brain. I was told to return in 10 weeks to see if it was gone. The doctor said that if it was not gone, then we would have to discuss the options at that time. When I got to my car, I told God I needed to hear from him in this situation. I opened my bible to Psalm 37:5 which says, *"Commit thy way unto the Lord, trust also in him; and he shall bring it to pass"* (KJV). I heard the Holy Spirit say to me "What is your it"? I said, "Lord, my "it" is I want this cyst gone." I simply heard him say, "I will." Every day, I said out loud "He will" because faith comes by hearing. I needed to hear it repeatedly so that my faith would come to the level of a miracle. A few weeks later, I was sitting in a drive thru and I looked at the license plate on the car in front of me. The license plate read "He will." It was as if God was speaking right to me, and I knew he had answered my prayer. I went to have a scan when ten weeks had passed and the cyst on her brain was gone. Praise God!

Many times, I have thought about how God used this pregnancy to challenge my faith. There is a saying, *"You don't need a miracle until you need a miracle."* Because I desperately needed a miracle for my unborn child, God used it to test my faith. If I was going to receive a miracle, I needed to make a choice to believe in God despite the results of the scan that day. I had to decide that though I believed "God can," I did not want to be left with the possibility that the cyst could be gone. I needed the certainty of knowing it would be gone. So, that day, I made the conscious decision to step out of my comfort zone and step into faith that produces miracles.

Restoring Faith in Miracles for the Next Generation

It is time to restore faith in miracles for the next generation. To do this, it is also time to return to the practices that the generations before us proved to be effective in seeing the miraculous. Practices like fasting which unlocks spiritual power you simply cannot get any other way. There is power in denying oneself to allow the Holy Spirit to have full control. Practices like getting back to prayer meetings. The bible states in Matthew 18:20, *"For where two or three are gather in my name, there am I with them"* (NIV). You cannot separate God's presence from his power. If he says he is there, his power is also there. Practices like consecration. To see God's miracle working power, the Church must be free of sin. Consecration calls for believers to set themselves apart from sin, to be holy as God is holy, to put aside every weight that so easily entangles us. Keeping the vision of miracles alive for future generations will require us to return to the practices that have been successful in the past.

In sharing what I have seen and experienced, my prayer is for generations to be encouraged to take hold of their faith, walk in the authority they have been given by God, and accept the call to govern His miracle-working power, making it evident again in today's church. I challenge every believer to not withhold your testimony of how you have seen God work. *Deuteronomy 4:9 states, "Only be careful, and watch yourselves closely so that you do not forget the things your eyes have seen or let them fade from your heart as long as you live. Teach them to your children and to their children after them"* (NIV). We have been instructed by God, tasked with teaching our children, our grandchildren, and future generations of the things we have seen God do. The torch was always meant to be passed so that God's miracle-working power would remain visible in the Church.

Because of the generations who came before me and accepted the call to steward God's miraculous power, instilling it for future generations, I still believe in miracles today.

Pastor Kimberly Robinson is the Assistant Pastor of The Saviour's House in Fayetteville, NC. She is the wife of David W. Robinson, Jr. They share two daughters. She is a second-generation preacher preceded by her mother, Pastor Sylvia Hardin Keller, and has been preaching the gospel of Jesus Christ for over 20 years.

21

GRACED TO TRUST

Turning the impossible INTO the POSSIBLE
Donna Rena Lowry

Life is full of challenges, some of which appear to be impossible. I have been no stranger to these kinds of challenges, but when I believe I am supposed to be doing something that God wants me to do, I determine that I am going to do it.

Such was the case when I felt that God wanted me to begin a business of caring for senior citizens. I had already completed my medical training, and while I was doing my clinical training, I saw clearly the path that I needed to take.

Over the course of the year, I attended monthly business counseling sessions at the Small Business and Technology Center in Fayetteville, where I was guided step-by-step on how to establish a business. These sessions required significant effort on my part, including extensive research at the library and countless hours at home on my computer, ensuring I conducted my due diligence. During this process, I remained in prayerful reflection, aligning my actions with what I believed to be God's direction.

I recall applying for licensure through the North Carolina Department of Health and Human Services, though it was known by a different name two decades ago as the North Carolina Division of Health Service Regulations. After submitting my application, I received a letter inviting me to schedule an appointment, provided I brought specific documentation. At the end of this meeting, I would be granted a license to open a home care company.

Excited about this progress, I shared the news with Mr. Greg Taylor from the SBTC, who had been instrumental in my journey. However, I soon encountered a roadblock: I needed a comprehensive policy and procedure manual to proceed. At the time, I barely understood what such a manual entailed, let alone how to create one.

A policy and procedure manual outlines the operational framework of a business, ensuring compliance with state and federal regulations. It also serves as a guide for licensure boards during inspections. Back then, this concept was entirely new to me. When Mr. Taylor referred me to a professional who could draft the manual, I was hopeful—until I learned the cost was $10,000, and the consultant stipulated that I could not open the business in Robeson County. This news felt like an impossible obstacle. Without the necessary funds and with no alternative location, I turned to God in prayer, placing the situation in His hands and trusting Him to guide my next steps.

I recall the prayer I prayed that was a little farfetched to my small thoughts at the time it sounded something like this: "Ok Lord, let's see how this is going to happen. Because I don't have access to $10,000 dollars. It was like a million dollars to me at that moment and where was I supposed to open the business if I couldn't start it up at the location God showed me which at the time was our kitchen table. How am I as a new startup company who is new in business with no funding and had no money saved secure another lotion that would have overhead cost like rent, lights, water, phone, office supplies and the list could go on." I had no other location in mind, but I was praying in that moment with doubt trying to figure this out in my mind. I immediately began running scenarios, ruling them out until it just didn't even seem possible in my mind. So, I simply said God I don't know how you are going to do this, but here you go. Looking back now I shake my head at the mere thoughts I had toward an impossible prayer.

Sometimes, we forget who truly *owns the cattle on a thousand hills*—the *King of Glory*. Today, I can boldly declare who God is, with the full authority of His Kingdom. He is the same God who parted the Red Sea when the children of Israel stood at a dead end, fleeing from Pharaoh and his army. He is the God who *spoke* the universe into existence, bringing order out of chaos. He is the same God who multiplied five loaves and two fish to feed over 5,000 people. And in Matthew 17:24-27, He instructed Peter to cast a hook into the Sea of Galilee, where Peter caught a fish with a coin in its mouth—just as God said he would—providing the means to pay their taxes. Now I know, with unwavering certainty, *With God, all things are possible.*

Less than two weeks later, I received an unexpected call from my father, James Jacobs Jr., who informed me he had found someone willing to write the policy and procedure manual for me. This person was Dr. Sherman Brooks, a respected individual my father had recently met when he was called to his home to fix his washing machine. My dad was one of my biggest cheerleaders and encouraged me as an entrepreneur. Daddy supported and encouraged my sisters and I to strive for success. Yes, you might think it was random, but I don't believe that it was a coincidence that God used my earthly father to connect me to the individual that blessed me with a policy and procedure manual by my heavenly father. A meeting was promptly arranged with Dr. Brooks.

That Monday evening, my husband, parents, and I visited Dr. Brooks' home. Upon arrival, I was struck by his warm demeanor and his willingness to assist. When he asked me why I wanted to open a home care company, I shared a pivotal experience from nursing school.

During my Emergency Room clinical rotations, I encountered an elderly man who frequently visited due to dangerously high blood sugar levels. Initially, I assumed his repeated admissions were a result of poor dietary choices. In my reports to my instructor, I would express that he simply needed to eat healthier. However, my instructor would gently remind me, "Donna, you don't know his story. You don't know his personal circumstances or the external factors contributing to his situation."

In my final semester, I was fortunate to complete a clinical home healthcare course, and it was no coincidence that this same gentleman became one of my patients. This was an encounter that would lead me to the Divine Destiny of my life. When I first saw his name on the assignment list, I immediately recognized it—it was the same patient from the Emergency Room.

Upon visiting his home, I came to understand the profound challenges he faced. He lived in poverty, was illiterate, and lacked access to essential resources. His home had no running water, and his pantry contained little more than canned beans, which he warmed on a small wooden heater. This experience profoundly changed my perspective, teaching me the importance of empathy and the critical role of understanding a patient's full story.

This encounter profoundly transformed my perspective. With the guidance of my instructor, I spearheaded efforts to improve his living conditions by arranging for running water, securing meal deliveries through the Meals on Wheels program, and coordinating home health services to assist with his insulin management. By the end of the semester, his quality of life had improved significantly.

It was in this moment that God said this is your destiny to establish a home healthcare business to support elderly individuals in similar circumstances, enabling them to live with dignity and proper care. I remember God saying you are to assist those in need with their activities of daily living by touching their hearts, thereby touching their lives, and that will touch their family. There, the seed was planted to establish a home care business dedicated to supporting elderly individuals facing similar challenges, enabling them to live with dignity and receive the care they deserve. It was during this pivotal moment that I embraced the company's motto: *"Touching hearts, lives, and families."* Grounded in the belief that assisting with daily living activities has a ripple effect—touching hearts, transforming lives, and positively impacting families—this vision continues to guide my mission in providing compassionate care.

After graduating from nursing school and gaining experience as a traveling nurse, I felt my steps being ordered by God and I was compelled to act on this vision. When I explained my situation to Dr. Brooks, he listened intently. I also shared my challenges with the $10,000 policy manual fee and the restriction on opening my business in Robeson County. Dr. Brooks' response was one of genuine support, marking the beginning of a breakthrough in my journey.

He asked if I had chosen a name for the company, and I replied, "Yes, sir. It's called *Caring Touch Home Health Care*, and God even inspired the perfect logo—praying hands," I said, holding up my hands as if in prayer. With a warm smile, he responded, "You can pick up your policy and procedure manual next Monday," then asked if I had any questions. I hesitated before asking, "Yes, sir, but what will it cost me?" His answer left me speechless: "Nothing. I'm writing it for you at no cost."

I could hardly believe my ears—free of charge! What I thought was impossible had been made possible. It was a powerful reminder of how God opens doors, even when none seem to exist. From that moment on, I knew with certainty that God not only was but *always* will be the one who transforms the impossible into the possible.

This experience taught me invaluable lessons about faith, perseverance, and the importance of trusting in God's timing and provision. Through obstacles and uncertainties, I witnessed the fulfillment of a purpose greater than myself.

"Trusting God to Use YOU as a Funnel to Channel Blessings to Others"

Are you READY to completely TRUST GOD to use YOU as a funnel to channel blessings to others, changing their Impossible to POSSIBLE?

Inspired by how Dr. Sherman Brooks was used by God to transform my impossible into the POSSIBLE, I committed myself to a similar mission. I wanted to serve as a vessel that God could channel blessings to others, dedicating my life to being used in whatever way He wills to impact and uplift those around me. First, I must share an example of a time when I partially walked in disobedience, and it came at a cost.

Occasionally, I would visit local churches for revivals to hear evangelists preach and minister in my hometown of Lumberton, North Carolina many years ago. One night while attending The Rock Church of God, under the leadership of Pastors Ronald and Alice Scott. I vividly recall Pastor Scott addressing the congregation before the evangelist began ministering. He encouraged those who were able to sow into the ministry of this traveling evangelist, who had journeyed a significant distance to share the Word of God. This offering was specifically designated for the minister, with Pastor Scott instructing us to write checks directly to him. He assured us that 100% of all funds collected would go to support the evangelist. As I reached for my checkbook,

I distinctly felt God prompting me to write a check for $5,000 dollars. I sat there, stunned, thinking, "$5,000? That's a significant amount of money." I found myself questioning, "In this small church, with such a large figure, God, are You asking me to give on behalf of everyone?"

Yes, I found myself questioning God about what to give, even though everything ultimately belongs to Him. In that moment I didn't remember how God used Dr. Brooks to freely write a policy and procedure manual for me that could have cost $10,000 dollars.

I wrote a check for $500 and placed it in the offering plate as it passed by. As I tucked my checkbook into my purse, I felt satisfied, thinking it was a generous offering. I assumed the evangelist, along with all the others who had contributed, would receive a significant sum. However, as the minister began to preach, the Holy Spirit began to convict me, reminding me that I had not followed His initial prompting. Throughout the service, I felt a persistent tug on my heart. I thought to myself, "What can I do now? The offering has already been collected, it's too late." In a moment of repentance, I prayed, "God, I was not obedient. Will You give me another opportunity? I promise ***I will listen and obey.***"

At the conclusion of the service, after the altar call and witnessing lives being transformed and souls saved, I remember Pastor Ronald Scott stepping back up to the microphone. He explained that although he typically does not take up two offerings, he felt led by the Holy Spirit to give someone an opportunity to sow into the Kingdom of God by contributing to the minister.

He opened the minsters Bible and placed it on the altar, saying, "Whatever you feel led to give, you may come and lay it here in the Bible. Once again, the Holy Spirit prompted me to write a check for $5,000. I began writing a check for $4,500. However, the Holy Spirit immediately corrected me, asking, "What are you doing?" I responded, "I'm writing the check for $5,000." The Holy Spirit replied, "No, you're writing it for $4,500." I then explained, "But I already wrote a check for $500." The Holy Spirit reminded me, "That was your decision, but I specifically instructed you to write a check for $5,000." I quickly voided the $4,500 check, turned to the next one, and wrote it for $5,000. With a sense of obedience, I walked up to the altar, folded the check in half, placed it in the Bible, and left.

It was only a couple of years later that I had the opportunity to witness the powerful testimony from a congregation in another state. As I listened to the Pastor's story, I was overcome with emotion, and chills that ran up and down my spine. This Pastor, shared a story of another evangelist whom he was acquainted with. He said this traveling evangelist was faithfully following God's calling, moving from place to place with his family, sacrificing along the way. Each relocation brought with it the burden of living expenses, car payments, insurance, and the pressures of daily life.

He had reached a point where, though obedient to God, he found himself in need of a divine intervention. Desperately, he prayed, "God, I need a sign tonight. I need a miracle. I want to serve You freely as an evangelist, without the constant worry of car payments or where my next meal will come from. I trust You, Lord, but I need something unbelievable. I need a clear sign that I'm on the right path."

He expressed to God with a pure heart, "If You move on my behalf and provide this sign, I will never doubt You again. I will know that I am doing exactly what You've called me to do. I want to continue ministering with my family, but I need help here in this small town, in the middle of nowhere. I need someone to walk into this service and write a $5,000 check."

> I know what you're thinking, how can you put a financial demand on God? When you are walking into your Divine Purpose, GOD WILL make provisions if you completely surrender your will to HIS WILL and TRUST HIM.

It was almost as though he made this request out of disbelief, not truly expecting such a thing to happen. In that humble, rural setting, he TRUSTED God for the impossible, thinking there was no way someone would come forward to give such a large sum. His request was not for a combined offering, but for a single $5,000 check—exactly what he felt he needed as a sign to continue evangelizing.

Does this situation sound familiar? Here I was, experiencing an opportunity to be used of God to bless someone else after launching my business successfully. God entrusted me with a seemingly simple task—a blessing for someone else. At that moment, I didn't even realize that I was being used to walk in obedience so that God could answer a prayer for this minister, enabling him to step into his anointing and DIVINE DESTINY.

It was one of those situations where I felt stunned. I said to God, "Wow, you're using me as a funnel to channel a blessing to someone else, but who am I? Just a little girl from a small little country town" all the while forgetting that this was something I had prayed for. I was so grateful that the Pastor didn't mention any names while sharing that story, as that moment wasn't about me receiving accolades for writing the $5,000 check. It was about God making provision.

All I could do was humbly cry at the altar, during the altar call, and repent once again, saying, "God, I'm sorry"—reflecting on that pivotal moment years ago. Had I heeded and followed God's instructions from the beginning, I would not have faced the loss of the $500 I hastily wrote in a check. However, the lesson I gained through this experience was truly priceless.

I shared this experience with the hope of encouraging you to COMPETELY TRUST GOD. There are moments when God's directions may seem unclear or even questionable, but obedience requires both faith and a willingness to TRUST the promptings of the Holy Spirit. Without that trust, the journey becomes far more challenging. This experience also deepened my understanding of stewardship. Everything we possess tangible or intangible—

1. *Tangible: Real Estate, Vehicles, Electronics, Jewelry, Precious Metals, Collectibles, Cash, Bank Accounts, Investments and anything that determines your net worth often recorded on a financial statement under assets.*

2. *Intangible: Intellectual Property, Brand and Marketing Assets, Customer-Related Assets, Content and Media Assets, Software and Technology Assets, Legal and Regulatory Assets, Organizational and Workforce Assets, Strategic and Financial Assets, Entertainment and Artistic Assets, Digital Presence and Online Assets, Community and Membership Assets and Miscellaneous Assets but not limited to Insurance claims and policies, Mineral rights, Water rights, Airspace rights, Royalty agreements (mining, oil, music).*

—belongs to God. We are merely caretakers of the blessings He entrusts to us during our time on earth. This realization profoundly shapes my perspective, reminding me that none of these earthly possessions can accompany me when I leave this life for my eternal home in heaven.

It is my heartfelt prayer that the lessons I have shared will inspire you to TRUST God more fully, to listen attentively to His voice, and to walk in obedience, knowing that His plans for you are always for your best interest.

> *"For I know the plans I have for you,' declares the Lord, 'plans to prosper you and not to harm you, plans to give you hope and a future'"* Jeremiah 29:11 (NIV).

Kingdom Entrepreneur

Donna Rena Lowry, a visionary entrepreneur and philanthropist, is the founder and CEO of Caring Touch Home and Behavioral Healthcare. With over 20 years of leadership, a U.S. patent, and numerous accolades, she blends innovation, ministry, and service, empowering her community and exemplifying excellence in both business and faith-driven initiatives. Donna is married to Charles Lowry, and together they have a daughter, Alexis.

22

GRACED TO WAIT

*Trusting God's Promises in a World
of Instant Gratification*

Prophetess Tracy Smith

Introduction:

In an era characterized by rapid technological advancements and a pervasive culture of instant gratification, the concept of waiting can often feel foreign and burdensome. Waiting is one of life's biggest challenges, and this is something most of us have challenges with, we need more patience. Everything we do now is at our fingertips, and while I love that, we could never have anticipated the instantaneous effect of getting things so rapidly in our world.

The desire for instant gratification permeates every aspect of life, from social media interactions to consumer habits, creating a collective impatience that challenges traditional spiritual values.

Yet, within the Christian faith, the act of waiting is not merely a passive state; rather, it serves as an opportunity for profound spiritual growth and deepened trust in God's promises.

There is a grace that God endows us with waiting as we navigate a world that prioritizes speed over substance. Often, we are being processed while waiting. The Bible is filled with many examples of waiting for God's timing. For example, David waited 15 years after being anointed by Samuel as Israel's next King. One thing is certain: faithfulness leads to divine fulfillment. It is essential to recognize that waiting, although challenging, can foster a deeper connection to one's faith.

Waiting on God's timing and promises is a spiritual prerequisite for spiritual and natural growth. Cultivating trust in God's timing (which is often challenging) requires intentional practices that align our desires with His will; thus, we must consider practical steps to embrace periods of waiting as transformative experiences rather than mere delays.

Several scriptures that have brought me through my most challenging times are the following scriptures:

> *"Wait for and confidently expect the LORD; Be strong and let your heart take courage; Yes, wait for and confidently expect the LORD"* (Psalms 27:14, AMP).

> *"I am GOD. At the right time, I'll make it happen"* (Isaiah 60:22, MSG).

Ultimately, recognizing the beauty inherent in these moments allows us to appreciate God's greater plan and encourages us to reflect on our spiritual journey through delayed fulfillment. God's grace empowers believers to wait patiently while nurturing our relationship with God (amid societal pressures for immediacy). However, one must acknowledge that this journey is not always easy, because it tests our faith. Although waiting can be difficult, it often leads to growth and a deeper understanding of who God is.

Understanding Grace in Waiting:

Understanding grace in waiting involves recognizing that this passive state is, in fact, a dynamic process through which individuals can cultivate deeper faith and spiritual resilience. In a society that prizes immediate results, the act of waiting can often be perceived as a burden rather than an opportunity for growth. God gives us the grace to have strength while we are waiting and trusting in his appointed time.

The Believers Struggle

Waiting on God poses significant challenges for believers, primarily due to the inherent conflict between spiritual expectations and societal norms. In a fast-paced world where instant gratification is the norm, the act of waiting can feel counterintuitive and uncomfortable. While waiting on God, we can feel powerless and unproductive because things are not moving on our timeline. Society has taught us everything is instant, and somehow, we have put that unrealistic expectation on God. The desire for immediate results clashes with the Bible, which calls for patience, creating an internal conflict that can be difficult to navigate. As believers, if we are not careful, we can become discontented and depressed during times of waiting. While some prayers are answered swiftly, many individuals endure extended seasons marked by unanswered requests, even times of suffering, which may last years or even decades. This reality emphasizes not only the difficulty in accepting divine timing but also underscores the necessity for perseverance and faith amidst uncertainty.

The pursuit of instant satisfaction often fosters impatience, which can undermine one's ability to trust in God's timing and promises but it is essential to recognize the importance of patience as it is vital for true spiritual development, although many may struggle with this.

I can recall when the Lord spoke to me about being in government. For years, I knocked on doors and nothing happened. I remained steadfast, believing in the word that God spoke to me. Decades later, I am now seeing the manifestation of that word.

Worldly impatience is characterized by a relentless pursuit of immediate gratification and control over outcomes, often leading to frustration and dissatisfaction. This form of impatience is deeply ingrained in contemporary society, where technological advancements perpetuate a culture that values speed more than anything else.

Social media affects our sense of reality and attention span. People see short snippets of videos and move on to the next. You are not seeing the process of the work of the individual by moving from one place to the next. This false perception affects a person's patience, their ability to have meaningful relationships because their lenses are eschewed, and they do not want to go through a process.

Biblical Exhortation to Wait on God

"Let us not grow weary or become discouraged in doing good, for at the proper time we will reap, if we do not give in." (Galatians 6:9, AMP)

We must continue our pursuit to not quit despite our delays and maintain our faith amidst uncertainty. Social media and our culture significantly shape our expectations for quick rewards and immediate feedback, often elevating our need for instant results. This relentless pursuit can impede our personal growth and hinder skill development, preventing us from reaching our true potential

"For I know the plans and thoughts that I have for you,' says the LORD, plans for peace and well-being and not for disaster, to give you a future and a hope." (Jeremiah 29:11, AMP)

God's plan for all our lives is not one of a disastrous future but one of hope. His nature reflects that He is Good! He is a good Father who is reliable, trustworthy, and faithful. His intentions are good for you, your family, and your nation. Waiting becomes an exercise in reliance on God's character. His faithfulness and commitment to fulfill His promises. This understanding is essential to our faith!

Moreover, understanding grace in waiting encourages individuals to view challenges through the lens of purpose rather than frustration. Each moment spent waiting can be seen as preparation for what God has planned: a time for spiritual refinement and personal transformation. Although this perspective shifts focus from immediate gratification, it causes us to become more reliant on God rather than man. Understanding this, God is not like man, he cannot lie, His promises are yes and amen! By cultivating this understanding, individuals can navigate life's uncertainties with confidence and peace fully trusting that their waiting will lead them closer to experiencing God's abundant blessings. Although exercising patience may be challenging, it serves a greater purpose.

Cultivating Trust in God's Timing, Trust the Foundation in Waiting

To cultivate trust in God's timing, one must engage in a deliberate effort to align expectations with the divine nature of God. This recognition that waiting is not merely a passive state necessitates an active engagement with faith. In a society that glorifies immediacy, believers often grapple with impatience; they question God's promises when fulfillment does not occur within their desired time. Trusting in God's timing requires understanding that His plans may differ significantly from human timelines. Biblical examples underscore this principle: figures such as Abraham and Joseph experienced prolonged periods of waiting before witnessing the fruition of God's promises.

Practical Steps

Embracing Waiting:

Embracing waiting as a spiritual practice involves several practical steps that help individuals navigate the tension between societal demands for immediacy and a deeper call to trust in God's timing. First, intentional prayer is fundamental. Engaging in regular conversations with God fosters a connection and reassurance during periods of uncertainty. Prayer is what I have built my life on; it has opened the door to the very presence of God! Prayer gives us the advantage over everything we face in life! Prayer is a time of communicating with God and allowing him to communicate with you.

Additionally, incorporating scripture into your daily prayer life can provide comfort and perspective; passages that emphasize God's faithfulness during times of waiting can reinforce trust in His promises. However, this process may require patience because not all individuals grasp the significance of these moments.

An essential step in waiting for God, in addition to prayer, is reflective journaling and being quiet in God's presence. These practices encourage believers to pause, reflect on their thoughts and feelings about waiting, and recognize God's presence in their lives.

Posture of Waiting on God

The distinction between passive waiting and actively engaging with God is critical for understanding spiritual growth and development. Passive waiting is often marked by inaction and a lack of purpose; this approach can lead to feelings of helplessness and negativity because individuals await divine intervention without taking proactive steps in their journey of faith. For instance, Moses illustrates this point. His years spent as a shepherd were not merely idle times but rather a period of preparation for his future leadership. In contrast, active waiting embodies intentionality and engagement with God's plans. However, one must recognize the importance of both approaches, although they differ significantly. Active waiting causes us to cultivate a posture of doing things, such as engaging in prayer and reading the word. This postures maturity and resilience and allows us to solely trust on God and wait on His timing.

> *"The Lord does not delay [as though He were unable to act] and is not slow about His promise, as some count slowness, but is [extraordinarily] patient toward you, not wishing for any to perish but for all to come to repentance."* (2 Peter 3:9, AMP)

> *"But those who wait for the LORD [who expect, look for, and hope in Him] Will gain new strength and renew their power. They will lift up their wings [and rise up close to God] like eagles [rising toward the sun]; They will run and not become weary, they will walk and not grow tired."* (Isaiah 40:31, AMP)

Attitude Matters

Growing up, my aunt engrained in me the belief that my attitude determined my attitude. Age-old wisdom underscores the profound impact of thoughts on our actions and overall well-being. Negative thoughts can lead to chronic stress and health issues, however, positive thinking fosters resilience and promotes success. We have heard an idle mind is the devil's workshop.

Our outlook not only determines personal satisfaction but also significantly influences future accomplishments. You can have whatever you say! Death and life are in the power of the tongue. We can shift our present! It's through our voice! It is through our mind. We have the mind of Christ! What are you speaking? What are you declaring? Are you speaking about life, or are you speaking about defeat? Choose life and speak the word only! Do not allow your negative thoughts to determine your next place!

Personal Testimony

For many years I stood on the promise of not only words but dreams the Lord gave me about working in government. I remember God showing and speaking to me that I would serve in government as early as age 16! I had my own timeline of when I thought this would happen. When it didn't happen, I dealt with a place of frustration, depression, and even second-guessing what God told me, even though I knew I heard God, everything was going contrary to what He had spoken. I had doubts and much unbelief, and during those times, I had to steal away. My action plan entailed me continuing to pray and knock on doors, I put my faith into work! I did not just sit on my hands to wait for things to happen. The result has been that not only am I working in local government, but my gift has also made room for me and brought me before great men.

Encouragement

My word to you is do not give up while in the desert! God will fulfill every word he has spoken over your life! I encourage you to employ the follow strategies while waiting on the promise of God

1. Pray/Fast
2. Meditate on the Word/pray the word
3. Have accountability partners

Unwavering commitment from God underscores His faithfulness and integrity, assuring us that regardless of external circumstances, His word remains dependable. Such assurance is essential for nurturing faith amidst life's uncertainties. Moreover, the way God fulfills His promises often transcends human experience.

God is reliable, trustworthy, and faithful! Hebrews 10:23

Prayer

Father, I pray that you encourage the heart of every reader as they wait to see the fulfillment of your word in a world of instant gratification. Let them not conform to the culture, but Father, let them realize that you are a good father. Let them know you give good gifts to your children. Let every form of delay be broken off their lives. I pray that they will be resilient in their pursuit after you! Let them be unwavering, bold, and courageous as they wait upon you! Let them realize you are the Sovereign God, and your promises are yes and amen. The thoughts you have toward them are good and not evil, so help them release everything into your hands. There is nothing that is too hard for you. Let their perspective begin to shift and let them begin to frame their world with your word! Let them release the victim mentality and exalt you, who is the only one in control! Let delay be broken, and let answers come expeditiously. I decree they will not faint in the waiting, but the grace and strength of God will come to propel them to their Next! §§§

Tracy Smith is a faith-driven leader, strategist, and community builder with over 20 years of experience in real estate and business consulting. As a governmental prophet, HR Director, and mentor, she blends innovation, empathy, and prayer to inspire others, uplift communities, and ignite purpose through Tracy Smith Ministries.

23

GRACED TO LIVE

Teach Us to Number Our Days
Pastor Darrel Geddes

> "So teach us to number our days, that we may apply our hearts unto wisdom."
>
> — Psalm 90:12, KJV

A Life Well-Lived

When I think of living life well, my first thought goes to the life of my mother, Marguerite Maude Burton Geddes, who graced this earth for **105 years and 363 days.** She exemplified to me a well-lived and well-loved life. Her legacy as a mother, grandmother, great-grandmother, friend, and spiritual mentor touched the lives of many. Her wisdom, faith, and devotion to God challenged the lives of all of us in her community in the light of eternity.

Marguerite's life called us to embrace the truth of Psalm 90:12, which invites us to live intentionally, with wisdom and reverence for God. Her passing prompted questions that every person must confront:

- What happens when I die?
- Is there really a heaven or hell?
- Where will I spend eternity?

Marguerite's life offered an answer to these questions. Through her relationship with Jesus Christ, she prepared for eternity, leaving behind a blueprint for us to follow. This chapter explores what it means to "number our days" and live with wisdom in light of God's eternal plan.

Considering Who God Is

"Before the mountains were brought forth, or ever thou hadst formed the earth and the world, even from everlasting to everlasting, thou art God." (Psalm 90:2, KJV)

To understand the brevity of life, we must first acknowledge the eternal nature of God. God is not a myth or invention of human imagination. He is the Creator of all things (Genesis 1:1), the sustainer of life (Colossians 1:17), and the One who desires a personal relationship with us (John 3:16).

God's Eternal Nature

The Psalmist contrasts God's everlasting existence with the fleeting nature of human life. While mountains and earth have beginnings, God is eternal, unchanging, and sovereign. This perspective humbles us and reminds us that our days on earth are limited. Understanding who God is brings us hope that transcends the temporal. John 3:16 promises eternal life through faith in Christ, reminding us that death is not the end but the beginning of eternity with God. Marguerite's life reflected this hope. Her prayer life, marked by intercession for her family, was rooted in her belief in God's power and faithfulness. She understood that her life was a vapor (James 4:14), but her prayers would leave an eternal legacy.

Remembering Who We Are

"The days of our years are threescore years and ten; and if by reason of strength they be fourscore years, yet is their strength labour and sorrow; for it is soon cut off, and we fly away." (Psalm 90:10, KJV)

Man's Mortality

Human life is brief and filled with challenges. James 4:14 describes life as a vapor that appears briefly and then vanishes. Whether we live 70 years or more, the reality of death confronts us all. Marguerite's life exemplified this truth, as even her remarkable 105 years came to an end. According to Biblical literature, the longest-living human being was Methuselah. Genesis 5 says that he lived to the ripe old age of 969 years. He had almost a thousand years of life, but he eventually died. And we are no different! My Mom lived to the ripe old age of 105 years and 363 days! I can't tell you how many people have remarked to me and my siblings about her long, lucid and primarily healthy life! Scripture suggests that our lives may endure between 70 and 80 years. Mom added 36 years to that total. As mom got older and her health began to fail, she would let anyone who would listen know that she was ready to transition. On one occasion, she called each of us and informed us that this was her last day on earth and that the Lord was going to take her, so you can imagine how disappointed she was when she awakened the next day. It was only at her end when she began suffering with congestive heart failure that she began asking us who was holding on to her. I told her Mom, no one is holding on to you, God is just not finished with you yet.

Man is Born to Die

The inevitability of death reminds us of our need for spiritual preparation. Hebrews 9:27 declares, *"And it is appointed unto men once to die but after this the judgment"* (KJV). This sobering truth should drive us to live intentionally and seek God's will. Despite her long life, Marguerite was ready for her eternal home. Her readiness came not from the number of her years but from her relationship with God. She often spoke of her longing to transition to heaven, showing us how to embrace life's brevity with faith.

Applying Our Hearts to Wisdom

"The fear of the Lord is the beginning of wisdom: and the knowledge of the holy One is understanding." (Proverbs 9:10, KJV)

Wisdom begins with reverence for God. This fear is not terror but respectful submission to His will. By acknowledging God's sovereignty and aligning our lives with His purposes, we gain a heart of wisdom.

Foolish Living

Youth often brings a sense of invincibility, leading us to ignore God's guidance. Ecclesiastes 12:1 urges us to *"Remember now thy Creator in the days of thy youth"* (KJV), for life's brevity demands that we live wisely, not foolishly. Marguerite's salvation at age 57 marked a turning point. Her transformation demonstrated the power of submitting to God's will and living with intentionality.

Practical Preparation for Eternity

Just as we prepare for unforeseen events—buying insurance, saving for retirement—we must prepare for eternity. Marguerite's decision to follow Christ in 1975 secured her eternal destiny and gave her peace in her later years. *"Behold, I stand at the door, and knock: if any man hear my voice, and open the door, I will come into him, and will sup with him, and he with me"* (Revelation 3:20, KJV). A personal relationship with God is the foundation for numbering our days wisely. Religion alone cannot save us; only a relationship with Jesus Christ can transform our lives and assure us of eternity with Him. On October 11, 1974, I entered into a personal relationship with Christ. I was radically transformed as a result of entering into that relationship. My mother and father saw the radical change and contributed it to me becoming a part of and being under the control of a cult. My mother was so concerned that she decided to investigate the church that I was attending, "Faith Temple Church of God in Christ" in Evanston, Illinois.

At 57 years of age, she walked with me from our home at 82nd and Blackstone to the bus stop on 82nd and Stony Island Ave. and we rode it down to 63rd Street, where we went to the Jackson Park Howard train from the South side of Chicago to Howard Street that divides Chicago from Evanston. We then got on the Purple Line at Howard Street and took it to Dempster, and walked from Dempster to 1932 Dewey about a good mile and half.

She sat down and enjoyed the service with me and at the end of the service Bishop Moody gave an invitation for those who would like to enter into a personal relationship with Jesus Christ. To my surprise my little petite 5'1' mother went forward and invited Jesus to come into her heart as her Lord and Savior. Marguerite's salvation experience demonstrated her willingness to embrace this relationship. Her life thereafter was marked by prayer, devotion, and a deep love for God and others.

Steps to Salvation:

1. **Acknowledge Sin:** *"For all have sinned, and come short of the glory of God."* (Romans 3:23, KJV)

2. **Confess Sin:** *"If we confess our sins, he is faithful and just to forgive us our sins."* (1 John 1:9, KJV)
3. **Accept Jesus as Savior:** *"For whosoever shall call upon the name of the Lord shall be saved."* (Romans 10:13, KJV)

A Legacy of Wisdom and Faith

If Marguerite could somehow speak to us today, her gentle encouragement would echo the words of scripture: *"Teach us to number our days, that we may apply our hearts unto wisdom."* If all of her family were able to plead with her to come back and remain here with us, I believe Mom would respond in that soft gentle voice, Oh how I love you, but its better for me here. I will not return but I would encourage you to 'number your days' so that you can see me again.

> "Blessed are the dead which die in the Lord… that they may rest from their labours; and their works do follow them." (Revelation 14:13, KJV)

Rev. Darrell John Geddes, Sr., pastor of Christ Church International in Minneapolis, MN, has over 37 years of ministry experience. A North Central University graduate, he has pastored in Chicago, Little Rock, and Minneapolis. Rev. Geddes is a leader in urban ministry, a General Presbyter of the Assemblies of God, and a proud husband, father, and grandfather.

24

GRACED TO PERSEVERE

Don't Stop Don't Quit

Apostle Dr. Royal McClinton

*"I can do all things through Christ which strengthened me." (*Philippians 4:13, KJV)

"And let us not be weary in well doing for in due season we shall reap, if we faint not." (Galatians 6:9, KJV)

My late spiritual mother, Apostle Nina Marie Leslie, once wrote me an encouraging note that I read every day during my devotions. She wrote:

"Dear son, you are full of purpose and full of My design, says the Lord. Your pieces that were once broken are fitly joined together. I love you; I created you and framed you into the jovial person you are. I never desired for your insecurities to overwhelm you; they were there for you to triumph over them. I wanted to show you your strength and abilities. Fear not of failure, for I have called you triumphant, so embrace the new."

"P.S. You will succeed. Love, your Father."

Throughout the ups and downs of my life, I cannot count how many times I wanted to quit—whether it was drinking my stress away or contemplating ending my life. That process started at the early age of seven after my dad died. I was so mad at God because I felt, "Why did He have to take him from me while my other friends had their dads?" Yes, I questioned God, and at that time, I never received an answer.

I never received counseling; I was just told to keep living and everything would be okay. I gave up on school and just went through the motions. As long as I didn't fail a grade, I felt no one cared, so I didn't care. My stress relief from the age of seven to seventeen was fighting—finding a reason to fight, getting suspended so I wouldn't have to go to school. I basically quit school without officially quitting.

I did find mental relief in high school by playing football. I discovered that I had to maintain a C average to be eligible to play, so I did just enough to get by. I had coaches who saw something in me and kept me encouraged. They talked to me to understand why I acted out as I did. They would say, "Your mother didn't raise you that way because your older brothers don't act that way." My answer was always, "I'm my own person; I'm not them"—just excuses.

My coaches always yelled at me, "McClinton, don't stop! Don't quit!" Those words stuck with me, even today as I share my story. Moving forward, my thinking changed as I gave my life to Christ, got married, had children, and developed a different outlook on life. I realized God had His hands on my life even during my tests and trials. I recognized that despite my struggles, He is always with me, reminding me through notes from my spiritual mom, my wife, children, grandchildren, church family, family, and friends.

I became a football, baseball, and basketball coach. I loved encouraging young boys, including my son who reminded me of myself. I wanted to pour into them as my coaches did for me. I encouraged them to keep pushing and keep striving despite circumstances. My rally cry was, "Don't stop! Don't quit!" My goal was to build their confidence and abilities through sportsmanship, whether they won, lost, or drew.

Through the years, I learned that you cannot reach your goals if you stop, quit, or put yourself on pause. Time truly waits for no one; you would look up and have regrets if you stop and quit. My favorite scriptures are Philippians 4:13 and Galatians 6:9. Every time I read and study those scriptures, the Holy Spirit reveals something different.

As I'm writing this chapter, I want to encourage you: when you go through your tests and trials, it's not enjoyable, but it is purposeful. God has a plan for you (Jeremiah 29:11). These challenges teach you to build your faith and trust in God and instill discipline. So, I encourage you today, if you are ready to give up, remember what Mama Nina wrote to me:

> "God never desired for your insecurities to overwhelm you; the test is there for you to triumph over them "

In closing I would like to talk to our young people who feel like quitting and giving up, whether it's school, work, marriage, life.

#1 TRUST GOD, He is our Hope.

#2 BELIEVE IN YOURSELF, when life gets stressful encourage yourself, you are a winner, and you are more than a conqueror.

#3 YOU SHALL LIVE and NOT DIE; you are born with a purpose.

#4 PRAY, PRAY, PRAY!

#5 EXPECTATION, your prayers will be answered in God's timing trust the process, and

#6 ALL YOUR NEEDS WILL BE MET!!!!

Don't stop! Don't quit!

Apostle Dr. Royal McClinton, Senior Leader of Life in Christ Family Worship Center International, brings over 30 years of ministry and security expertise. Co-author of *Bare Naked and Not Ashamed: The Marriage Manual*, he ministers uniquely to those in need and leads Royal Security & Transportation Services. Husband, father, and grandfather.

AFTERWORD

Govern With Grace

As we conclude our journey through this anthology, I am deeply grateful for the opportunity to have shared these reflections on divine, self, and kingdom governance with you. It is my fervent hope that the stories and teachings presented in these pages have not only enlightened but also inspired you to step into the fullness of the authority and grace God has bestowed upon you.

Reflecting on the lives of God's faithful servants, we have seen how their alignment with His divine governance has transformed not only their lives but also the lives of those around them. This transformation is a testament to the power of living under God's sovereign rule, dedicated to fulfilling His purposes.

As you move forward from this reading, carry with you the profound understanding that to govern effectively in any capacity, one must first be governed by the Almighty. Let this truth permeate every aspect of your life, influencing how you lead, serve, and love those in your sphere of influence.

May the lessons of governance you've learned here inspire you to act justly, love mercy, and walk humbly with your God (Micah 6:8). And as you do, may your life serve as a beacon of His grace and truth, a living letter known and read by all whom you encounter.

Thank you for allowing these pages to be a part of your spiritual journey. May you go forth with the courage to govern wisely and the assurance that you do so under the watchful eye and loving hand of our Sovereign Lord.

God bless you richly as you govern with grace.

Dr. Deborah C. Anthony

Made in the USA
Columbia, SC
29 January 2025